Clues to Acting Shakespeare

Clues to Acting Shakespeare

WESLEY VAN TASSEL

ALLWORTH PRESS
NEW YORK

04 03 02 01 00   5 4 3 2 1

Published by Allworth Press
An imprint of Allworth Communications
10 East 23rd Street, New York, NY 10010

Cover design by Douglas Design Associates, New York, NY

Page composition/typography by Sharp Des!gns, Lansing, MI

ISBN: 1-58115-022-9

LIBRARY OF CONGRESS CATALOGING-IN-PUBLICATION DATA
Van Tassel, Wesley.
Clues to Acting shakespeare: skills clarified for the actor, student, and reader / Wesley Van Tassel.
p.   cm.
Includes bibliographical references (p.) and index.
ISBN 1-58115-053-9
1. Shakespeare, William, 1564–1616—Dramatic production. 2. Acting. I. Title.
PR3091 .V36 2000
822.3'3—dc21
00-024397

Printed in Canada

In America, the struggle for media success often reduces the art of acting to the act of marketing.

"Nothing will come of nothing . . . ,"
Lear observes suspiciously.

Playing Shakespeare has nothing to do with marketing and everything to do with the art of acting.

FOR DUDE,
who is so very good at this!

THIS BOOK HAS FOUR PARTS:

1. For Actors in Training: Acting Shakespeare
Part 1 is designed for college classes or independent workshops and includes a complete study of ten basic skills required to play Shakespeare's language truthfully. This section is designed for a training period of twenty to thirty weeks meeting four to eight hours per week. Actors may also use this material to self-teach.

2. For Secondary Schools: Reading Shakespeare Aloud
In part 2, some of the skills from part 1 are condensed for high school English or drama teachers and their students and are also useful for reading groups.

3. For Professional Actors and Coaches: The One-Day Brush Up
For the actor preparing an audition or a role—or the coach or director brushing up—part 3 is a quick review of four essential skills.

4. Resources
A collection of exercises, an annotated list of selected successful and not-so-successful film and video performances, a bibliography of some excellent books, a glossary of terms, and the index.

Bait the hook well! This fish will bite.
MUCH ADO ABOUT NOTHING, II, iii

Contents

Part One: For Actors In Training: Acting Shakespeare

Emphasis in Actor Training • The Realistic Actor • The Classical Actor • The Film Actor • Are These Skills Difficult to Learn? • Know Thyself • Identifying Common Mistakes • The Big "Character" Mistake • What Goes Wrong? • Why the British Seem Better at This • Two Approaches to Training • Better Training • What Are the Special Skills? • What About Meaning? • What If These Skills Are Too Difficult? • To Summarize

Ten Basic Skills • Required Text • What is Blank Verse? • What is a Regular Blank Verse Line? • What Are Feminine Endings and Elision? • What is a Short or Shared Line? • What is a Rhymed Couplet? • What Are Scansion and Stresses? • How Do I Select the Breathing Points? • What is a Caesura? • Text Study Seems Academic: Does It Matter?

Part Three: For Professional Actors and Coaches: The One-Day Brush Up

Part Four: Resources

I will arm me, being thus forewarned.
HENRY THE SIXTH, PART 3, IV, i

Acknowledgments

To CICELY BERRY, for the published account of her work with the Royal Shakespeare Company, a huge debt is gratefully acknowledged. She has shared her discoveries brilliantly through her acting and voice books, notably *The Actor and the Text* (Scribner's, 1988), which is one of the best books on acting ever written.

Together with thousands of other actors, directors, and coaches in America, I am grateful to John Barton for producing his invaluable *Playing Shakespeare* text and accompanying videos (Methuen, 1984).

I am indebted to Kristin Linklater, especially for her *Freeing Shakespeare's Voice* (Theatre Communications Group, 1992), Delbert Spain's study, *Shakespeare Sounded Soundly* (Capra, 1988), Edward S. Brubaker's *Shakespeare Aloud* (Author, 1976), Robert Cohen's *Acting in Shakespeare* (Mayfield, 1991), and Patsy Rodenburg's *The Need for Words* (Routledge, 1993), all of which in their different ways affirmed what I have been doing the past twenty years.

Special thanks to Penguin Books for permission to quote from *The Complete Pelican Shakespeare* (Alfred Harbage, General Editor).

My gratitude is expressed to the following persons who read the manuscript and made invaluable contributions: Don Perkins (Actor, New York and Williamstown Theatre Festival); Patricia Norcia-Edwards (Rutgers University, M.F.A. Program); Joel Fink (Roosevelt University, M.F.A. Program, Chicago, and the Colorado Shakespeare Festival); Bonnie Raphael

(University of North Carolina at Chapel Hill, M.F.A. Program); Sandy Robbins (University of Delaware, M.F.A. Professional Actor Training Program); Harris D. Smith (University of Nebraska, M.F.A. Program); Scott Hayes (Florida State University, Asolo Theatre Conservatory, M.F.A. Program); Fred Goodson (Director and Elmira College Theatre Program Chair, New York); Charles Leader (Actor and Chair, Kansas City Community College Theatre Program); Leslee Caul and Michael J. Smith (Central Washington University Theatre Program); Jennifer Bennett (Actress, Washington); Nedra Dixon (Actress/Director, New York); Wendy Waterman (Tisch School of the Arts, New York University, Collaborative Arts Project); Jon Kerr (Pierce College, Washington); Laurie Kash (Sunset High School Drama Program, Beaverton, Oregon); Clint Pozzi (Actor and Drama Director, Meadowdale High School, Seattle); Nola Boughton, Robert Pierce and Anna Thorpe (Conroe High School, Texas); Zoe Climenhaga and Miriam Climenhaga (Bisbee Community Theatre and Cochise College).

Special thanks to actors David Plant, David Shoup, Kerri Van Auken, Keith Edie, and David Foubert, who helped introduce the manuscript to readers; to Nance Bracken for the graphics; and to Jen Huszcza, video librarian at the New York Public Library for the Performing Arts. Special thanks to Neil Freeman, University of British Columbia and editor of the modern-type *First Folio Editions* of Shakespeare. Together with the persons listed above, eleven teachers in a 1999 summer workshop made wonderful suggestions for part two. My thanks to Chris Carey (Huntington High School, Oregon), Katherine Carey (Eastside High School, Covington, Georgia), Hendrea Ferguson (Newberg High School, Oregon), Jim Fewer (Marshfield High School, Coos Bay, Oregon), Brian Hanson (Choteau High School, Montana), Leeann Mueller (Tenino High School, Washington), George Obermiller (West Valley Junior High School, Washington), Chris Pierson (Port Townsend High School, Washington), Jay Thornton (Enumclaw Junior High School, Washington), and Kate Wilson (Olympic College, Washington).

Special thanks and appreciation are expressed to Allworth Press publisher Tad Crawford, my editor Nicole Potter, her editorial/production assistant Jamie Kijowski, and their staff, whose excellent work on the book makes me look better!

And finally, my thanks to the several hundred actors and actors in training who I've had the pleasure to coach in "acting Shakespeare." You are too many to name, but you know who you are! Those hours were both a great pleasure and a special privilege for me, and I hope they were for you!

Condemn the fault, and not the actor of it.

MEASURE FOR MEASURE, II, ii

Introduction

It shall do you no harm to learn.

ALL'S WELL THAT ENDS WELL, II, ii

The intention of this book is to help the working actor discover and use specific skills for acting Shakespeare. There are many books *about* acting Shakespeare, but most deal with historical, philosophical, or personal approaches to the characters. They offer interpretations of these characters that are often drawn from actual performances (e.g., Antony Sher's *Year of the King*). But for the working actor struggling with blank verse, only a few of these books are of "immediate" or practical value. Several voice studies that illustrate the union of Shakespearean text and developed vocal skills are the most useful.

When preparing to act a role, the actor must learn to handle the language of the specific play so that the character will be truthful in both intention and presentation. Heightened language, as in Shakespeare's plays, can be difficult, and failure to handle it effectively will quickly destroy an otherwise well-intended characterization. Therefore, the actor must train the voice and then learn specific *skills* to handle this language. Once these skills have become practice, books that talk about *acting* Shakespeare are very helpful for character research and analysis.

That few books are available to help the working actor gain the skills necessary to handle verse is not surprising. A coach or director cannot write about this process until he or she has worked with hundreds of actors and discovered successful techniques.

I have had the privilege to coach the skills presented in this book to several hundred professional and student actors. These actors, mostly American, *taught me* that what they needed most were skills to handle the language, especially the verse, as those skills would allow them to play characters truthfully. Most of these actors expressed confidence about character intention and development (the skills that are the core of realistic actor training), but were uncomfortable with the idea of playing their characters while speaking verse. Most of these actors were amazed (and then delighted) to learn that with Shakespeare, the character is discovered *through the verse.*

Therefore, when coaching Shakespeare, one must always begin with the practical skills required to speak the text. The scope of this book is limited to that study. Techniques to develop the character that emerges from correctly speaking the text are the subject of other books, many of which are listed in the bibliography. *Character study must always follow language study.* With Shakespeare, the reverse spells disaster, as I will clarify in these pages.

This book is primarily for actors who intend to play Shakespeare but whose training is based on realism. Because that specific training rarely considers blank verse, you, the actor, are probably missing a few skills. These skills must be identified and learned so that your work with Shakespeare can be successful.

When using this book, professional actors should turn immediately to part 3, page 129, the "Professional Actor's One-Day Brushup" for a quick review of skills you probably already know. Actors in training or professionals who want more detailed study should begin with part 1. Secondary teachers, reader groups and community theatre groups should begin with part 2, page 85, and refer back to part 1 as necessary.

Some of the realistic acting skills that you apply to Chekhov, Williams, Miller, Wasserstein, Mamet, or the dialogue in most films are important and applicable to acting Shakespeare. For example, once you've trained your voice, *playing your action to achieve your objective* is still the most important acting skill. But some of the others, like reading the subtext or emotional memory recall, are less important than the language when playing Shakespeare.

Special skills required to play Shakespeare must be *added to* or *replace* what you've already acquired. The differences are not in motives, actions, personalities, relationships, or conflicts (the ingredients of character and plot), but in the requirements of the language.

Two excellent studies on acting heightened text and acting realism are, respectively, Cicely Berry's *The Actor and the Text* and Constantine Stanislavski's *An Actor Prepares*. The subjects are often similar and share many common truths, yet certain skills are very different and will be identified in this book. While nothing needs to be changed in either Berry or Stanislavski and every actor should master what each teaches, these exceptional works share a common problem: Their great depth of information can confuse and discourage the reader. The confusion is especially evident among American actors who attempt to master unfamiliar techniques for acting Shakespeare through Berry's book, unless they are fortunate enough to have an excellent coach who is familiar with the skills. Without a personal coach, or with a coach who is learning along with the actor, how does the actor trained in realism prepare to learn these many new approaches to acting?

Clues to Acting Shakespeare clarifies the specific preparation and identifies the skills required to act heightened text—to move from Chekhov to Shakespeare—to adjust from one language structure to the other. Procedures for learning these skills are included. The skills also apply to acting Shakespeare's contemporaries, other verse drama like Molière or the Greeks, and to modern realistic text.

Advanced study should follow, beginning with *The Actor and the Text* and Barton's *Playing Shakespeare* book and video series. Correct vocal usage should be learned and practiced, using the techniques of Berry, Kristin Linklater, or Patsy Rodenburg. When you are ready for a much more detailed study of verse structure, refer to Delbert Spain's *Shakespeare Sounded Soundly*.

Clues to Acting Shakespeare will not deal with playing realism— for example, Stanislavski's methods, Meisner, Hagen, and so on— because it assumes the reader has experience in that field and is now taking the step to act heightened text.

I have spent nearly twenty years coaching "acting Shakespeare" at universities or private workshops and even longer directing his plays. This book has evolved into a summary of what actors have taught me over the course of these decades. I hope these "clues" simplify the process for you and help make the material accessible. Don't let Shakespeare's text frighten you. This greatest of writers wrote *for actors*, and discovering what you can do with this language is challenging, stimulating, all-consuming, rewarding, and great fun!

He was skillful enough to have lived still.
ALL'S WELL THAT ENDS WELL, I, i

For Actors in Training: Acting Shakespeare

Now name the rest of the players.

A MIDSUMMER NIGHT'S DREAM, I, ii

CHAPTER I

Common Understandings

Their understanding
Begins to swell, and the approaching tide
Will shortly fill the reasonable shore.

THE TEMPEST, V, i

BEFORE WE BEGIN work on the specific skills required to act Shakespeare, let's review and clarify some terms and approaches to acting. Answering these questions now will give us a common foundation for the exercises that follow.

EMPHASIS IN ACTOR TRAINING

The Realistic Actor

The term "realism" refers to realistic scripts that are written in prose, where dialogue reads like everyday speech. Included are most stage plays written after 1900 and nearly all film and television plays. "Realistic actor" refers to that individual who has studied the craft primarily to act realistic text by application of Stanislavski methods. "Realistic actor" may suggest an artist who has taken supervised voice study, but that assumption may or may not be true. At any rate, it would be unrealistic to assume that any actor proficient in realism would automatically be a skilled presenter of Shakespeare.

The Classical Actor

The phrase "playing Shakespeare" refers to the performance of plays written in heightened language. Heightened text follows specific rhythmic patterns and is usually filled with imagery. Included are most plays written prior to

3

1900. There are exceptions, like Chekhov, Strindberg, and Ibsen, who wrote realism. Generally, learning to handle Shakespeare's heightened language also gives the actor a solid foundation for playing Molière, Restoration comedy, Goethe, Rostand, and many others. As most of these plays are referred to as "classical," actors trained to perform them are often called "classical actors."

The Film Actor

Nowadays, we also have the "film actor." This additional category is necessary because many performers on film are certainly "actors," but they may or may not possess the training and skills that stage actors acquire. Actors, including persons identified as "stars," who work primarily on film or video may or may not have a trained voice, and may or may not be capable of a range of characterization.

These categories actually identify an actor's training and preparation to work in the profession. The profession itself has many forms—stage, classical stage, musical stage, dance, video, film, radio, spoken books, recordings, voice-over, sales shows, demonstrations, modeling, and so forth. Well-trained actors can work in most of the forms, whereas less talented or less trained persons might specialize.

In this book, our concentration is on performance of Shakespeare's plays for stage, video, or film. However, many of the skills required to perform this task successfully can be applied to acting realism and other performance opportunities—indeed, they should be applied whenever possible.

ARE THESE SKILLS DIFFICULT TO LEARN?

O, answer me! Let me not burst in ignorance.

HAMLET, I, iv.

No, but they must be learned. When an actor trained in realism tackles a Shakespearean role without applying these special skills, the usual results are an affected voice and strained and unbelievable acting. Shakespeare's language controls the actor, rather than the actor controlling the language. The ability to play realism on film or stage does not translate to the ability to play Shakespeare.

But, since fine Shakespeare acting coaches are available, actors with some degree of talent can be successful at playing verse. When we observe unsuccessful performances, we are left to wonder: (1) Where were the coaches? or (2) Is that actor really without talent?

The skills required for success with Shakespeare, once explained, are not hard to recognize. For example, young actors in training are often shown film or video performances of Shakespeare's plays. These student actors can quickly articulate the reasons for good or poor performances.

Part 4 lists some selected film and video performances that contain interesting acting challenges and are well worth studying.

KNOW THYSELF

Now will I begin your moral, and do you follow.

LOVE'S LABOUR'S LOST, III, i

As a realistic actor approaching Shakespeare, you face specific challenges; therefore, you must know your starting point. If you are a *strong realistic actor,* you probably work somewhat in the following way: You develop a character through playing your action and discovery of subtext and objectives. You realize that your action has to be measured in the person from whom you want something. In the rehearsal process, you find ways to "use" the text to illustrate and play your actions. Speaking the subtext, especially in many modern plays, is, you realize, often as important as speaking the actual words. You have success with these techniques, your character dominates the language, and you control the situation. This approach gives you strength and believability.

If you are a *limited realistic actor*—perhaps with little or no training or an ineffective voice, without the natural skills required to be honest—you can't work within this framework, because you can't speak the subtext or play the action truthfully. You may have a "tin ear." That problem is usually compounded by an untrained voice and a tendency to apply sarcasm to each line reading.

I believe that the application of sarcasm is rampant amongst poorly trained American actors, and I'm sure you have heard it in the performances of others. For truth, personality is substituted, and for honest feelings, attitude. The actor colors the text with sarcasm, thinking the text needs coloring, and not knowing what else to do or how else to do it. Many actors with limited skills can be seen daily in videos and television programs. Trained actors and directors recognize this limitation. Untrained actors and directors (and producers and casting agents) think such actors are just fine—as long as they are marketable.

Whether you are a strong or a limited realistic actor, you can easily identify the skills required to perform Shakespeare. You must then determine for yourself if you can go beyond identification to the process of learning and applying these skills.

IDENTIFYING COMMON MISTAKES

Awake your senses, that you may the better judge.

JULIUS CAESAR, III, ii

The First Mistake: When a realistic actor approaches Shakespeare by asking, How shall I play this character? the first mistake has been made. Instead, the actor must ask this question: What is this language doing and what is the action implied?

The Second Mistake: Assuming that a character can manipulate the language is the second mistake. In realism, you play the subtext and sometimes can establish your own rhythm. In Shakespeare, the meter and rhythm are set for you, and you must play accordingly.

The Third Mistake: Plunging right into character development is the third mistake. When studying a Shakespearean role, development of character is the third thing you do, not the first. The first is text analysis, and the second is speaking the language aloud; only then can you make choices about what the character is doing and saying.

The early development of character choices is a serious mistake made by nearly all actors (student or professional) who attempt to play a character that is written in heightened language. The reason for the mistake is understandable: Realistic actor training is based on methods to discover truthful character, so it is difficult to refrain from immediate character choices.

THE BIG "CHARACTER" MISTAKE

When reading a script, actors imagine characters and quickly search for actions to bring those characters to life. Text study can seem to delay the opportunity to play the character. Many actors don't realize that with heightened language, character discovery comes *through the text*. These actors believe that text study is an intellectual activity that has little to do with playing the role. When acting Shakespeare, that naiveté will spell disaster.

If you know some basics about music and decide you want to play the piano, how successful will you be if you don't learn the skills? If you want to play baseball, but prefer to ignore hitting and fielding practice, how good will you become? Without applying yourself to master the skills, how successful can you be at anything?

But once you become really good at something, skills move to the background and your mastery of the activity takes over. We refer to such a performance as "effortless." We, the viewer or listener, see no technique—only skillful results. How much effort does it take to make something "effortless?"

Unless you make the effort to discover what the language is saying and doing, and then have the skills to read that language correctly, your Shakespearean characterization will be unsuccessful. Regardless of the amount of time you put into development of the character, if you haven't first discovered what's in the words, your character cannot be completely engaging; the audience will not clearly understand you and won't quite believe what you are saying.

WHAT GOES WRONG?

Pause awhile
And let my counsel sway you in this case.
MUCH ADO ABOUT NOTHING, IV, i

Everything. But primarily this: When you develop character *first,* you then tend to "adjust" the language to fit what the character wants to do, and you say the lines "the way the character would say them."

This approach spells disaster, because you are deciding *how* to say the lines before you know *what* you are saying. This Stanislavski acting principle is especially true when acting Shakespeare: Know *what* you are saying and *why* you are saying it, and the *how* will take care of itself.

The importance of Stanislavski's advice is *amplified* with Shakespeare, because, when compared to realistic text, the *what* is much harder to determine. When reading a blank verse line, you have a greater chance of being entirely wrong in your interpretation of what is being said, in which case, nobody will have any idea what you are saying.

You may have noticed, when watching Shakespeare, that the British actors, especially on film, sound much better than the Americans. Are they better actors? No. Are they better at Shakespeare? Yes. They are better trained to handle heightened text.

WHY THE BRITISH SEEM BETTER AT THIS

Thus comes the English with full power upon us.
HENRY V, II, iv

We often hear the argument that American actors will be better at Shakespeare if they use a British accent. John Barton argues convincingly in his book *Playing Shakespeare* and the accompanying videotapes that skill in handling Shakespeare has nothing to do with accent. He also points out that, when comparing American and British accents, the American is probably closer to actual Elizabethan speech. The American sound is rougher, less refined, more authentic.

And yet, when Americans approach Shakespeare for the first time, both professional and student actors seem to add this vocal affectation. This application (or coloring) not only weakens the voice, it destroys all chance at truth and honesty of character. Use your best and strongest natural speaking voice when handling Shakespeare's language.

TWO APPROACHES TO TRAINING

The primary reason why British actors are better than American actors at playing Shakespeare is simply the method of training.

The British start actor training with voice and movement, plus scene and language study. Many American training programs, acting schools, and studios begin with inner motivation, self-discovery, and characterization. It can be argued that the American system of actor training should be reversed: Teach Shakespeare performance with its required skills first, then teach realistic acting technique.

If this reverse were realized, Americans would have an earlier opportunity to play Shakespeare, and there would be no difference between British and American actors. Then why don't we do it?

The reverse isn't practical for the American job market. Work for actors in America is 99.5 percent in realism and 0.5 percent in plays with heightened language. American children are raised on television and film, so they are familiar with realistic text and acting styles long before actor training begins. Except in studio work or school, an American actor might work an entire career and never have a shot at a Shakespearean role.

Dustin Hoffman, one of America's best actors, reached the age of fifty-one without ever having played Shakespeare. His opportunity came when he played Shylock in Sir Peter Hall's production of *The Merchant of Venice* in 1989.

Of necessity, the business side of acting attracts American actors to realistic training, which is where the roles are.

In England, the foundation of most regional theatres is the Shakespeare canon, and the plays are included in every season. His plays are also produced extensively at the various festivals in England and Canada and at the Royal National Theatre in London. School children perform the plays in grade school and see numerous productions. Most actor training programs are independent and not housed in universities, as they are in America. Most British acting coaches see Shakespeare training as mandatory. The classic repertoire of British drama is in heightened language. In

England, an actor cannot avoid Shakespeare training; in America, the actor must search for it.

Recent trends in England, however, such as the job market in film and television and declining funding which leads to a declining number of classical stage productions, indicate that British actor training is showing an added emphasis on the American approach.

When rehearsing American actors for two Los Angeles Shakespearean productions in 1999, Sir Peter Hall was asked by the trade newspaper *Back Stage West* if he rehearsed longer than he would have in England.

> A little more. But to tell the truth, the tradition is not in a healthy state in Britain now either, because there's not enough Shakespeare being done there, because drama schools don't teach actors something they're probably never going to do. So I don't even do a Shakespeare play in England now without two weeks of teaching before I start. It wasn't all that different here, just a bit longer. (Scott Proudfit)

The "classic" repertoire of American plays is realistic or musical. When the Stanislavski techniques emerged in the 1920s, they were absorbed within ten years into American theatres and schools. Extensive training in voice, movement, and script analysis are recommended in Stanislavski's writings. But his early disciples in America largely ignored these techniques and favored concentration on motivation, sense memory recall, subtext, objectives, the magic "if," self discovery, etc.—in other words, the basic tools these teachers and directors believed were required to act the realistic texts that American playwrights were writing.

BETTER TRAINING

Let your reason serve
To make the truth appear where it seems hid.
MEASURE FOR MEASURE, V, i

The simple reality is this: An actor trained in Shakespeare performance can easily adjust to realistic text for stage or film. On the other hand, most actors trained in realism, especially for film, have no idea how to adapt that training to Shakespeare. In fact, the actor's training can actually hamper success. Except for the practical side of "making a living," it would make sense to reverse actor training in America. Is acting a business or an art?

Experimenting with the reversed training procedure, I have coached a half-dozen or so groups in which beginning actors (about age seventeen) were mixed with professionals, many of whom had numerous Broadway and LORT (League of Resident Theatres) credits. In these groups, the professional actors performed "final projects" at a higher level, but they did not learn the specific Shakespeare skills any faster than the beginners. One can conclude that the skills are easy to identify and learn, and that other factors like voice training and experience determine the level of performance.

A few M.F.A. acting programs now concentrate training on classical text. I have no doubt that young actors could be trained even earlier and, if started with voice work and the skills required to play Shakespeare, would graduate better prepared for the entire range of job opportunities.

WHAT ARE THE SPECIAL SKILLS?

Assuming an actor has a trained voice, the skills needed to play Shakespeare truthfully are:
* Learning to phrase and support the language
* Having the freedom to speak while playing your action

The first skill is tied to analysis of text, the second to voice and character.

WHAT ABOUT MEANING?

It is not especially difficult to study Shakespeare's language and explain its common meaning. As understanding improves, the actor is able to "dig deeper" and find more possibilities. One's knowledge and skill at the moment of reading a text are always changing, and among writers, Shakespeare especially seems to change.

Each time we come back to take a fresh look at a speech, we're amazed at the new ideas Shakespeare somehow inserted into the text since our last reading! We also begin to realize that the layers are infinite and that we will always discover something new.

Once the actor has a trained voice, the goal is to discover what's in the language and speak freely. What's in the language is discovered by learning and applying some basic skills to the blank verse. If the listener is actively engaged, the actor is using the correct verse skills.

Some directors believe that there are no rules applicable to performing Shakespeare, but that idea is certainly untrue. Specific skills needed to handle the language must be thought of as rules. If the actor ignores these skills, most listeners do not understand what is being said and simply doze off.

How long can an actor hold an audience that can't hear? The same is true if they can't understand, and all the work put into discovering the language and character will go unrewarded.

Discovering what the language means, and then having the skills to *speak* that discovery, is what separates actors from English professors. I've heard dozens of English teachers and professors read Shakespeare aloud, but the only ones I have heard read effectively are actor-trained. This problem reflects a misunderstanding about drama—plays are written to be spoken aloud. Speaking and acting skills are required for the listener to hear what the language is doing. Lacking these skills and still reading aloud is a sure way to confuse the listener.

As all actors know, an idea (or interpretation) in one's head doesn't transfer automatically to the audience's ears. That step takes special skills with any text, and Shakespeare is no exception. In fact, plays written in heightened text require far more speaking skills than realistic plays.

Director Peter Brook coined a wonderful phrase applicable to unclear actors and confused listeners: *"The trouble with Shakespeare is that it goes on without you."*

WHAT IF THESE SKILLS ARE TOO DIFFICULT?

Sir, I am too old to learn.

KING LEAR, II, ii

Who would attempt to sing an aria in public without first learning something about voice and music? To handle the technical challenges in the aria, the singer must have the instrument (the voice) and training (the skills). One could certainly sing the aria and ignore the composer's notations, but then the listener is cheated out of hearing the music's real possibilities. The performance is less than satisfactory, because the material has been "adjusted" to the singer's limitations. Untrained listeners, of course, don't know the difference.

"Adjusting" the material to fit personal strengths and weaknesses is what some actors do all the time. We usually refer to these performers as "personalities" rather than actors.

Philip Bosco, the fine American character actor, remarked in an interview about preparing to act Shakespeare in *In Theatre* magazine that "fame doesn't give you talent." An actor may have a pleasing personality on film and be paid a lot of money, but may not be equipped with the essential skills, especially a trained voice, to handle Shakespeare or other classics.

If an actor without correct preparation accepts a Shakespearean role, the necessary procedure is to secure a coach and learn the skills. Simultaneously, the actor must develop the voice to handle the language.

Shakespeare's plays are often cut or "arranged" for specific situations. These changes are the director's or producer's production choices, but not usually language changes. Refrain from rewriting Shakespeare's language to accommodate your personal vocal limitations as, for example, you might transpose a song to better fit the vocal range of a singer.

Instead, develop your skills to act what the language requires. If you are not willing to learn the skills, avoid Shakespeare, spare the audience the boredom, spare yourself the bad acting, and don't insult the author.

TO SUMMARIZE

O Lord, I could have stay'd here all the night
To hear good counsel: O, what learning is!

ROMEO AND JULIET, III, iii

What we want to do, then, is handle the language so that the audience clearly understands the character's intentions. We know that the more skillful we become at speaking the language, the more the audience will be involved.

Now let's begin on the specific skills.

USEFUL IDEAS TO REMEMBER:

CHAPTER 2

The Basic Skill Set for Working with Heightened Language

THERE ARE TEN basic skills required to play Shakespeare. Some are identical to the skills required to act realism.

TEN BASIC SKILLS

1. Play your action and achieve your objective.
2. Stay in the moment, listening, not thinking ahead.
3. Use scansion, phrasing, and the caesura.
4. Support the thought all the way through the line. The end of the line is often as important, or more important, than the beginning.
5. Breathe at the correct places.
6. Let the words be the expression of your thoughts. Do not think, then speak. Speak what you think when you think it.
7. Understand the speech structure and rhythm.
8. Play the antithetical words, phrases, and thoughts. Use the caesura to help you. These skills will clarify your phrasing and prevent you from rushing.
9. Use analysis to understand all words and thought patterns.
10. Love the imagery.

These skills will be studied one by one. All actors know that skills are to be mastered and "forgotten," then revisited during rehearsal. In performance, the moment and the action must take over. Most actors would rather be "involved in the moment" than engaged in the "chore" of text study. Not surprisingly, then, it is more difficult to learn the skills and apply the discipline needed to practice them than it is to forget the skills and allow the moment to take over.

From the above list, number 1, "play your action," and number 2, "stay in the moment," are the same skills used in acting realism. We won't spend time reviewing them.

So pause awhile . . .

REQUIRED TEXT

At this point, you need to choose two sections of Shakespearean text: (1) a monologue in blank verse (not prose) and (2) a sonnet. Ten or twelve lines are enough for the monologue, and these can be cut from a longer monologue. Pick a sonnet you enjoy.

Your selections will probably be regular lines—ten syllables in each—but you may have to adjust to feminine endings or short or shared lines. Rhymed couplets are fine. Scan the lines, mark the feet and stresses, note the elision, circle the caesuras, the breathing places, and the words that break the rhythm.

I just used a series of words and instructions that you may not understand. Before I explain the ultimate exercise, "kick the box," we'll take a detour and learn these terms. You'll soon be on your feet and working aloud.

WHAT IS BLANK VERSE?

My tongue could never learn sweet smoothing word.

RICHARD III, I, ii

Simply stated, it is unrhymed verse usually written in lines of ten syllables. This line structure is called *iambic pentameter.* An *iamb* is a foot (or word) of two syllables, the first unstressed and the second stressed.

An *iambic pentameter* is a line of verse that consists of five metrical feet—in this case iambic feet, so we have ten syllables per line.

Here's a blank verse line from *Hamlet*, spoken by Horatio about the Ghost, with the feet separated and the stresses marked: ∪ for unstressed syllables; / for stressed.

Horatio: It beck / ons you / to go / a way / with it,   (i, iv.)*

Walk around and think of your foot falling "heel toe, heel toe, heel toe, heel toe, heel toe," and count five feet with ten "syllables." The "heel" is unstressed and the "toe" is stressed. The stresses in verse are often defined "dee dum dee dum dee dum dee dum dee dum." Keep walking and substitute "dee dum" for "heel toe." That's the rhythm of blank verse.

Blank verse was developed by Shakespeare and his contemporaries in the late sixteenth century and is usually considered the written form closest to actual English speech. You speak blank verse all the time, usually without realizing it. For example, "What do you want to do this afternoon?" and "Let's go to town and buy an ice cream cone" are two lines of blank verse! Converse for awhile in blank verse, and write out a few original lines of your own.

Use this space to write a few lines of original blank verse:

WHAT IS A REGULAR BLANK VERSE LINE?

A regular line is comprised of ten syllables with alternating stresses: "Dee dum dee dum dee dum dee dum dee dum." In a regular line, the stressed syllable is always the second syllable of each foot. This definition will lead us to suspect that there may be lines which are not "regular." That is true and, in fact, is a key to how Shakespeare's language works. He will change the regular rhythm and catch the listener's ear. Learning to recognize these changes and handle them convincingly is a key to speaking this language. We'll work on that soon. The blank verse form is used in modern daily life and in classical dramatic text and poetry. Invent a few more blank verse lines for practice.

> *I pray you mar no moe of my verses*
> *with reading them ill-favoredly.*
> AS YOU LIKE IT, III, ii

---

*All line quotes are taken from *The Complete Pelican Shakespeare*, Alfred Harbage, General Editor. New York: Viking Penguin, 1977.

WHAT ARE FEMININE ENDINGS AND ELISION?

A blank verse line is sometimes spoken with eleven syllables rather than ten. The final syllable is not stressed and remains soft. The most famous line in Shakespeare illustrates the added syllable, the "dee" without the "dum," as Hamlet contemplates action.

Hamlet: To be, or not to be—that is the question: (*Ham*, III, i)

In this blank verse line, there are eleven syllables. The final syllable, the feminine ending, is a soft and unstressed syllable. The line scans like this:*

$$\breve{\text{To}} \text{ be,} / \text{ or not} / \text{ to } \breve{\text{be}} \text{— } / \text{ that is} / \text{ the ques} / \text{ tion:}$$

To recognize the feminine ending, you must count the syllables in the blank verse line. If you count eleven and notice that the final syllable would not be stressed—like "tion," "ing," or "en,"—you have a feminine ending. If you count eleven (or perhaps more) syllables but note that the final syllable must be stressed, you cannot use the feminine ending. In this case, use elision—contracting two words or syllables into one, like "I'll" from "I will"—to establish ten syllables.

In the following example, in which Hamlet speaks to Horatio with an eleven-syllable line, Shakespeare has already elided a two-syllable word into one, but the reader must elide another word, as "man" is stressed and would not make a feminine ending.

Hamlet: Horatio, thou art e'en as just a man.   (*Ham*, III, ii)

Note "even" is already elided to "e'en" and pronounced as one syllable. The actor must elide "Horatio" to "Horat'o," pronounced as three syllables. Now the line can be spoken in ten syllables with correct rhythm.

$$\breve{\text{Hor}} \text{ a} / \text{ t'o, thou} / \text{ art e'en} / \text{ as just} / \text{ a man.}$$

Elision is used frequently in Shakespeare. Here are more examples. In the first, Shakespeare provides the elision:

Gloucester: As flies to wanton boys are we to th' gods;   (*Lr*, IV, i)

*Some actors prefer: / that is / the ques /tion

Note that the fifth foot has three syllables, even with "th'gods" elided. This is acceptable and does not harm the meter.

$$\breve{\text{A}}\text{s flies} / \text{to want} / \text{on boys} / \text{are we} / \text{to th'gods;}$$

In the following examples, the actor must determine the elision:

Lady Macbeth: He brings great news. The raven himself is hoarse

(Mac, I, v)

Elide "raven" to "rav'n," spoken as one syllable; however three sounds in the fourth foot also works.

$$\text{He brings} / \text{great news.} / \text{The rav'n} / \text{him self} / \text{is hoarse}$$

Caesar: Nor heaven nor earth have been at peace to-night.   (*JC*, II, ii)

Elide "heaven" to "heav'n" spoken as one syllable.

$$\text{Nor heav'n} / \text{nor earth} / \text{have been} / \text{at peace} / \text{to night.}$$

Ghost: Cut off even in the blossoms of my sin,   (*Ham*, I, v)

Elide "even" to "e'en," spoken as one syllable.

$$\text{Cut off} / \text{e'en in} / \text{the blos} / \text{soms of} / \text{my sin,}$$

To elide or not to elide can be a confusing choice. If necessary, seek guidance or check the BBC Shakespeare video series. If no help is available, choose the way that sounds best to your ear, while keeping the rhythm.

As clear
As morning roses newly washed with dew.
THE TAMING OF THE SHREW, II, i

WHAT IS A SHORT OR SHARED LINE?

A short line consists of fewer than ten syllables. If the line is finished by the following line, usually spoken by the next speaker, it is a shared line. If not finished by the next line, the missing syllables are probably a direction from the author instructing the actors to take a pause before continuing.

For example, here's Bassanio in *The Merchant of Venice* begging Portia's forgiveness for the "lost" ring. His speech ends with a short line which she finishes with her first line. Then she ends her speech with a short line which he finishes. Generally the actor who finishes a short verse line has a quick cue to keep the rhythm.

Bassanio:	Portia, forgive me this enforced wrong;
	And in the hearing of these many friends
	I swear to thee, even by thine own fair eyes,
	Wherein I see myself,—
Portia:	Mark you but that!
	In both my eyes he doubly sees himself,
	In each eye, one. Swear by your double self,
	And there's an oath of credit.
Bassanio:	Nay, but hear me: (v, i.)

Here is another example. In Juliet's second of three exits in the balcony scene in *Romeo and Juliet*, she first speaks a short line which he finishes, then a short line which is unfinished and certainly calls for a pause as he watches her leave. Does the pause call for a kiss?

Juliet:	Tomorrow will I send.
Romeo:	So thrive my soul,—
Juliet:	A thousand times good night! *(exits)*
Romeo:	A thousand times the worse, to want thy light! (ii, ii.)

In the first two lines, his "So thrive my soul" finishes her "Tomorrow will I send." His second line, "A thousand times the worse, to want thy light!" is a regular verse line, and therefore it is not intended to complete her unfinished second line.

So there is an unfinished two feet after "A thousand times good night!" A four-syllable pause to be filled—a "dee dum dee dum." How? A kiss? A cross to the door and turn back? A cross and run back? A cross and thrown kiss? A hand clasp? A hand kiss? Just an exit? Your choice.

Farewell, farewell! One kiss and I'll descend.
ROMEO AND JULIET, III, V

WHAT IS A RHYMED COUPLET?

Just what it sounds like. Here are examples from *A Midsummer Night's Dream,* in which all of the verse rhymes and dozens of rhyming couplets can be found.

Helena: O, that a lady, of one man refused,
           Should of another therefore be abused!   (II, ii.)

Another:

Hermia: So far be distant; and, good night, sweet friend.
           Thy love ne'er alter till thy sweet life end.   (II, ii.)

Play the rhyme, don't try to cover it up. There is great pleasure in speaking and hearing it.

You will notice that your sonnet, and all of the other sonnets, ends with a rhyming couplet.

I have spoke the truth.
ALL'S WELL THAT ENDS WELL, V, iii

WHAT ARE SCANSION AND STRESSES?

Marking the soft and stressed syllables in a blank verse line is called scanning the line, or scansion. In a regular blank verse line, the second syllable of each foot is stressed, as shown on page 15. Shakespeare, however, achieves effects by creating irregular lines. In the following example, lines 1, 2, and 4 are usually considered regular, while line 3 is irregular. These are the opening four lines in *Romeo and Juliet.*

Chorus: Two households, both alike in dignity,
          In fair Verona, where we lay our scene,
          From ancient grudge, break to new mutiny,
          Where civil blood makes civil hands unclean.   (*Pro*)

Using regular scansion, in the third foot of line 3, the word "break" would not be stressed. For the sense of the line, however, your common sense tells you that the verb "break" is more important than the preposition "to," so the stresses are inverted and the line scans like this:

$$\breve{} \;/\; \breve{} \;/\; /\; \breve{} \;\breve{} \;/\; \breve{}/$$
From an / cient grudge / break to / new mut / i ny,

The third foot is called a trochaic foot, or trochee, as opposed to an iambic foot. The first syllable is stressed and the second unstressed, and the rhythm is broken. With just a little practice, you will learn to recognize irregular stresses and words that break the rhythm.

HOW DO I SELECT THE BREATHING POINTS?

It's easy to know when to breathe in Shakespeare; it's hard to make yourself do it. Breathe at the natural stops—the punctuation points—and not at the end of a verse line simply because, on paper, it looks like the end of a line. In verse, many lines are *enjambed*, which means the "thought" implicit in the line runs on from one line to the next without a break (or punctuation). In the above four lines from the *Romeo and Juliet* prologue, each line ends with punctuation, and you can breathe comfortably. But end-of-line breathing is usually *not* the case. In the following example, select the breathing points.

> Mercutio: O, then I see Queen Mab hath been with you.
> She is the fairies' midwife, and she comes
> In shape no bigger than an agate stone
> On the forefinger of an alderman,
> Drawn with a team of little atomies
> Over men's noses as they lie asleep;   (*Rom*, I, iv.)

Notice the enjambed lines. You would not take a breath after lines 2, 3, or 5. Circle the correct breathing points—after "O," "you," "midwife," "alderman," "asleep"—and memorize them at the same time you work on and memorize text. You will discover that breathing correctly actually helps you memorize. While inhaling physically, you mentally "inhale" your next line. While exhaling physically, you "exhale" the line. This technique is studied in more detail in chapter 5.

WHAT IS A CAESURA?

Pronounced si-zhoor´-ə, it is a "sense" pause, usually in the middle of a blank verse line. Some verse lines contain punctuation, others do not. On the ones that do not, a sense pause is almost always present. Mark it like this: //.

A sense pause does not mean a breath pause. Don't breathe at the caesura unless the breath is planned and necessary.

Look again at the lines of Hermia and Helena in the rhyming couplet section on page 19. In each case, their first line contains punctuation and their second line does not. In each second line, we can insert a caesura.

Helena: Should of another // therefore be abused!
Hermia: Thy love ne'er alter // till thy sweet life end.

Note the elision by the author of "ne'er" from "never," creating a one-syllable word. Shakespeare sometimes elides consonants, although elision of vowels is more common.

By using the caesura, the lines are broken into separate phrases. Separate phrases identify separate thoughts. Identifying thoughts clarifies the lines. We'll work more on phrasing and caesura in chapter 3.

TEXT STUDY SEEMS ACADEMIC: DOES IT MATTER?

The red plague rid you
For learning me your language!
THE TEMPEST, I, ii

Text study matters, because the structure matters. Compared to music, the structure is the notation. Compared to baseball, the structure is the hand-eye coordination. You've got to put it together if you're going to hit the ball.

USEFUL IDEAS TO REMEMBER.

Scansion, Phrasing and Caesura

In the previous chapter, we defined each of these terms. Now we'll look at them in greater detail.

SCANSION

Here is our simple modern-day blank verse line scanned. Each two syllables comprise one foot, and the soft and stressed syllables are marked.

$$\breve{\text{Let's}}\ \acute{\text{go}}\ /\ \breve{\text{to}}\ \acute{\text{town}}\ /\ \breve{\text{and}}\ \acute{\text{buy}}\ /\ \breve{\text{an}}\ \acute{\text{ice}}\ /\ \breve{\text{cream}}\ \acute{\text{cone.}}$$

Let's go / to town / and buy / an ice / cream cone.

Here's a better line from *Romeo and Juliet*.

Romeo: But soft! What light through yonder window breaks?   (II, ii.)

Break the line into feet:

But soft! / What light / through yon / der win / dow breaks?

Mark the stresses:

But soft! / What light / through yon / der win / dow breaks?

When you read the line, place emphasis on the stressed syllables: "soft," "light," "yon," "win," "breaks." With your hand, beat out these stressed words or syllables on the table or chair. Read the line a few times by beating out and *over-stressing* the five stressed words or syllables, then forget the scansion and read the line naturally.

If you've beat out the rhythm with your hand and emphasized the stressed syllables, you will discover that when you "forget" scansion and read the line more naturally, you automatically give a slight emphasis to the stressed words. Your goal is to achieve naturalness and honesty, but to do so by stressing the correct words.

For the Shakespearean line to be truthful, it is necessary to play the correct stresses. Let's test this idea by reading a line incorrectly. Here's the opening line from *The Merchant of Venice*.

Antonio: In sooth I know not why I am so sad.   (I, i.)

In sooth / I know / not why / I am / so sad.

If we follow the scansion, the stresses are "sooth," "know," "why," "am," and "sad." Read the line instead by stressing "In," "I," "not," "I," "so" and see what you get. That's probably not what you want!

For anything so overdone is from the purpose of playing.
HAMLET, III, ii

So pause awhile …

Now you need a pencil, not a pen. Put this book down and mark the scansion in your monologue and sonnet. Then read them aloud a few times, hitting the stressed syllables. Overdo it. Pound it out. You can pull back to realism later.

By overdoing, you discover meaning and "problems." Are there problems? Likely there are, so let's find them. For example, is there a stress that seems wrong? Or is there a line that won't scan to ten syllables? Trust your common sense, and remember that Shakespeare obtains much of his effect by inverting stresses, which changes the rhythm of the line. He will also write eleven syllable lines, sometimes with feminine endings, and, on occasion, lines of twelve to fourteen syllables. Here are examples that may be similar to your material.

Remember the *Romeo and Juliet* line from chapter 3?

Chorus: From ancient grudge, break to new mutiny,

The line scans like this:

From an / cient grudge / break to / new mut / i ny,

An action verb like "break" actually breaks the rhythm and creates a trochaic foot. Here's another example, as Juliet speaks to the Friar:

Juliet: Conceit, more rich in matter than in words,
           Brags of his substance, not of ornament.   (*Rom,* ii, iv.)

The line scans like this:

Con ceit, / more rich / in mat / ter than / in words,

Brags of / his sub / stance, not / of orn / a ment.

"Brags" breaks the rhythm. Often trochaic feet are found in the first foot of a line.

Here are regular lines and then a twelve-syllable line. Puck speaks to the Fairies in *A Midsummer Night's Dream*:

Puck: The King doth keep his revels here tonight.
         Take heed the Queen come not within his sight.
         For Oberon is passing fell and wrath,
         Because that she, as her attendant, hath
         A lovely boy, stolen from an Indian King.   (ii, i)

Four lines scan as regular, but in line 5, which has twelve syllables, we must elide twice—because "king" is not a feminine ending—and also discover a trochaic foot.

The King / doth keep / his rev / els here / to night.

Take heed / the Queen / come not / with in / his sight.

For O / ber on / is pass / ing fell / and wrath,

Be cause / that she, / as her / at tend / ant, hath

A love / ly boy, / stol'n from / an In / d'an King;

We have elided "stolen" to one syllable ("stol'n") and "Indian" to two syllables ("In-d'an"). "Stol'n" also breaks the rhythm. Now the line works.

Here are a few examples of feminine endings. In the first four lines of *Sonnet 58*, note that lines 2 and 4 have feminine endings:

> That god forbid that made me first your slave
> I should in thought control your times of pleasure,
> Or at your hand th' account of hours to crave,
> Being your vassal bound to stay your leisure.

The lines scan like this:

That god / for bid / that made / me thus / your slave

I should / in thought / con trol / your times / of pleas / ure

Or at / your hand / th'ac count / of hours / to crave

Be ing / your vas / sal bound / to stay / your leis / ure.

Note the elision in line 3.
Here's Iago in *Othello*:

Iago: And what's he then that says I play the villain,   (II, iii)

The eleven-syllable line scans like this:

And what's / he then / that says / I play / the vil / lain,

The "lain" of "villain" would not be stressed, so we know it's a feminine-ending line.

So pause awhile ...

In your monologue and sonnet, mark all words that break the rhythm, circle all feminine endings, elide as necessary, and check your initial scansion.

You discover changes in the rhythm by applying scansion and trusting your common sense. When the rhythm changes, play it. Once you are comfortable that your monologue and sonnet are correctly scanned, move on to "phrasing."

PHRASING

Phrasing means to break the verse line into individual thoughts. If you take any Shakespearean speech or sonnet, the obvious phrases are separated by punctuation. Paraphrasing Webster, for our purpose, a "phrase" is a group of words that create a thought on which the mind can focus momentarily, and which can be preceded or followed by a pause. As most actors know, it is easier to mark the phrases than it is to handle them vocally.

Here's an example in which most of the phrases are clearly marked by punctuation. In *Julius Caesar*, Brutus responds to Cassius's hint that Caesar has become too powerful.

Brutus:	That you do love me I am nothing jealous.	(1)
	What you would work me to, I have some aim.	(2)
	How I have thought of this, and of these times,	(3)
	I shall recount hereafter. For this present,	(4)
	I would not so (with love I might entreat you)	(5)
	Be any further moved. What you have said	(6)
	I will consider; what you have to say	(7)
	I will with patience hear, and find a time	(8)
	Both meet to hear and answer such high things.	(I, ii.) (9)

In lines 6–9, notice the phrases not separated by punctuation.

Here are those lines plus the next five. Caesuras (//) have been inserted to mark those phrases not already separated by punctuation. Some actors prefer to circle the phrases. Notice that the final four lines have no punctuation at all.

Brutus:	What you have said //	(6)
	I will consider; what you have to say //	(7)
	I will with patience hear, and find a time //	(8)
	Both meet to hear and answer // such high things.	(9)
	Till then, my noble friend, chew upon this:	(10)

Brutus had rather be a villager //	(11)
Than to repute himself a son of Rome //	(12)
Under these hard conditions // as this time	(13)
Is like to lay upon us.	(14)

The last is a "short line," calling for a pause or completion by the next speaker. In this case, Cassius finishes the line with "I am glad . . ."

Why bother to mark the phrases? Your goal is to know the phrasing of the line so that you can (1) separate the thoughts, (2) play one phrase against another, which is called antithesis, (3) allow a thought to continue to the next line, as needed, and (4) identify your breathing spots, just like singing.

Shakespeare uses antithetical words, phrases, or thoughts in nearly every speech. To handle this language, you must master playing antithesis, and this mastery begins with phrasing. For the actor, antithetical words, phrases, or thoughts provide clear insight into the meaning of the text. Antithesis is the subject of chapter 8.

So pause awhile . . .

Mark or circle the phrases in your monologue and sonnet. Now your scansion is nearing completion. Next add the caesuras.

Thus did he answer me, yet said
I might know more hereafter.
CYMBELINE, IV, ii

THE CAESURA

Nay, I'll speak that
Which you will wonder at.
ALL'S WELL THAT ENDS WELL, IV, i

The caesura, the short sense pause marked //, does many things:
- It allows the words preceding it to "sink in" before the listener must deal with more words
- It places focus on the word or phrase following it, giving that word or phrase special emphasis
- It slows the language down
- It separates phrases, which are often the character's thoughts, and allows the listener to hear them one at a time

When you run thoughts together, the audience is usually lost.

As with most rules, once learned they become automatic. Where caesura is concerned, use it thoroughly in rehearsal and preparation, as the use will force you to separate your thoughts. Then remove the caesuras, except where absolutely essential for audience understanding of a word or thought.

When the phrases are identified and the caesuras then removed, you will likely handle the line in such a way that each thought has its own emphasis and energy, and is clearly expressed without the pause. Using that pause in rehearsal, however, will guide you to the places where the thoughts separate.

Consider Richard's opening soliloquy in *Richard III*:

Richard: Now is the winter of our discontent
           Made glorious summer by this son of York;
           And all the clouds that lowered upon our house
           In the deep bosom of the ocean buried.   (i, i.)

We know that most verse lines without punctuation will take a caesura, usually somewhere in the middle. Arguably, you could place caesuras anywhere that thoughts change, or where you want to set up a word or phrase. Here is the same speech with lots of caesuras—far too many for performance.

Richard: Now // is the winter // of our // discontent //
           Made // glorious summer // by this // son of York;
           And // all the clouds // that lowered upon our house //
           In the deep bosom // of the ocean // buried.

Your Richard will not need these pauses, and indeed, the pauses will tend to make the speech jerky and indulgent. But each represents something special that is happening in the language. When you remove the pauses, following your discovery period in rehearsal—surely you must remove most of them for performance—you will automatically do something vocally or physically to clarify the possibility of each thought.

Ah, to be blessed with a strong voice and to have trained it! You will need it now as you remove the pauses, and yet, you must play each idea clearly and individually so that it reaches the listener's ear.

Most verse lines lend themselves to at least one caesura. Some already have the thoughts separated by punctuation, and additional caesuras may not be necessary. But the very structure of the blank verse line lends itself to division of thoughts and to "setting up" important words or phrases. Use the caesura, but don't be tempted to retain it anywhere, except where it adds to the listener's understanding. Speaking the language with correct rhythm is much stronger than speaking with pauses inserted for emphasis. Most caesuras are for discovery, not performance.

Here is another example from the same play. To overthrow Richard, Richmond says to his troops:

> Richmond: More than I have said, loving countrymen,
> The leisure and enforcement of the time
> Forbids to dwell upon. Yet remember this:
> God and our good cause fight upon our side;   (*RIII*, v, iii.)

You might separate the thoughts like this:

> More than I have said, loving countrymen,
> The leisure // and enforcement // of the time //
> Forbids to dwell upon. Yet // remember this:
> God // and our good cause // fight upon our side;

Line 1: The thoughts are already separated by the author.

Line 2: Play both factors—"leisure" and "enforcement"—not just one, and don't play both as one. Also, don't breathe after "time," but you might take a very short caesura, because you want to set up and attack the active verb "forbids."

Line 3: The thoughts are separated by the author in the middle of the line. "Yet" is one of many transition words used by Shakespeare (some others include "but," "then," "when," "therefore," and "or"), and you can use "yet" to set up the next idea. Do that here.

Line 4: The two factors, "God" and "and our good cause," should not be run together as one. Use them to set up the final phrase.

You are now deeply into the skills required to play Shakespeare!

And skills are exactly what we're developing. We haven't begun to tap our brains to analyze the possibilities of each thought. And yet the language will start to make sense if we simply use these speaking skills. They allow the language to be heard in such a way that the ideas are emphasized, even if we don't know what all of the ideas are. These skills alone will take you a long way in Shakespeare performance and in cold readings. You're starting to allow the language to live.

Sir John Gielgud made this remark: If you were not quite sure of a very difficult speech in Shakespeare and you studied the punctuation and got it right, the sense would in some way emerge (*Acting Shakespeare*, 35).

Now I begin to relish thy advice.
TROILUS AND CRESSIDA, I, iii

So pause awhile ...

Take some time to insert caesuras into your monologue and sonnet. Once done, your *basic* scansion is complete. It should include feet separated, stresses marked, words that break the rhythm circled, inverted syllables (trochees) identified, phrases marked or circled, caesuras marked, feminine endings and elisions noted, and preliminary breathing points circled. Later we will add antithesis, analysis, imagery, and more detail on breathing points. But for now, move on to "kick the box" and other skills.

USEFUL IDEAS TO REMEMBER:

CHAPTER 4

Support the Line and Thought

We'll begin these rites,
As we do trust they'll end, in true delights.

AS YOU LIKE IT, V, iv

THE ACTOR MUST support the verse line all the way through to the final word. An exercise I call "kicking the box" teaches this skill.* I began using this exercise when I started working with actors on Shakespearean text some twenty years ago—kicking first an eraser (which was too small), then a sweatshirt (which was too soft), then a soccer ball (which nearly broke the windows), and then settling on a cardboard box one day when we had no eraser or sweatshirt or ball.

KICK THAT BOX!

Let's first review *why* this exercise is so important, then we'll practice it. In coaching "realistic actors" to handle Shakespeare, I have found that kicking the box is the most effective way to learn complete support of the verse line. This is the most basic and simplest of all the skills, and yet it is one of the most important. It is so important, because the natural speech of American actors is dramatically opposed to this necessary skill.

A line of our everyday speech looks something like this:

---

*Cicely Berry, former voice coach for the Royal Shakespeare Company, mentions a similar exercise in *The Actor and the Text*, 179.

The emphasis and volume peak in the middle of the line, then fade away as if the speaker has lost interest in the thought or run out of breath.

In Shakespeare, the end of the line is equally important and many times more important than the beginning or middle, because it allows the thought implicit in the line to carry forward. As mentioned in chapter 2, many verse lines are enjambed, and the thought continues from one line to the next without punctuation or pause. In blank verse, the actor cannot afford to lose interest in the thought or run out of breath.

Kicking the box helps the actor support the final word or phrase and keep the thought from ending too soon.

We want to involve our entire body when speaking Shakespeare's language. Kicking the box helps the actor remain physically involved in the language.

For in such business,
Action is eloquence.
CORIOLANUS, III, ii

Supporting the last word or syllable of the blank verse line is not easy and, once learned, is easily ignored. Physiologically, our diaphragm doesn't want to work that way. The muscle is "lazy" and prefers relaxation to tension. During voice training, actors learn to use the diaphragm to support speech. But even after training, many actors forget to "kick the box."

They forget for three reasons:

- The effort to read the line "naturally" and truthfully encourages us to fade out at the end
- We don't practice speaking blank verse on a daily basis
- Breath support becomes lackadaisical, so rather than support the ends of lines, it is easier to allow them to fade away like they do in our daily speech

Because our vocal muscles are uncomfortable with a change, any effort to support the ends of lines may at first seem strange or "overdone." But supporting is correct. If you don't support the end of the verse line, one can project that your Shakespeare will not be clear or truthful. The listener won't quite know what you are saying.

You need great physical energy to speak Shakespeare's verse, and kicking the box helps you to remember to use your body. Energy is a key to your success. Remember, Shakespeare's plays were written to be performed:

- Outdoors
- In broad daylight
- For large audiences
- With much of the audience standing for the entire play
- With people sitting on stage
- Amid concession sales, like a baseball game
- With birds flying around
- With the audience talking back to the actors

If you try speaking in that setting, you will discover immediately how much vocal energy is required.

Here's the kick-box skill and how to do it.
In this example, Romeo is speaking to Friar Laurence:

Romeo: Thou canst not speak of that thou dost not feel.   (*Rom*, iii, iii.)

Scan the line. Now speak the line in a "natural" way, allowing the final word "feel" to fade away. The line works to a degree. But now, circle the word "feel." Place a small cardboard box on the floor and stand by it. Speak the line, and when you get to "feel," kick the box. Don't kick on "not," and don't kick after "feel." Kick right on the *f* of the word.

It may help if you take a split-second pause (a caesura) before "feel," as this allows you to position yourself and the word, and to get your leg and balance ready to kick—then kick. Later, forget the pause. It's only for the exercise.

You will notice that the kick does two things—it gets your body physically involved in speaking the language, and it gets you to support the word "feel." The intent here is not to overplay "feel," not to shout it, and not to call great attention to it. You simply support it, as opposed to letting it fade out.

Your ear should tell you that the line means different things when you support or don't support "feel." If you don't support it, Romeo seems to be telling the Friar not to "speak of things." That information is in the first half of the line. If you do support "feel," Romeo may be reminding the

Friar that he is celibate and has never felt the love of a woman, so how can he advise? That reading gives both actors much more to work with. Try it.

There are other interpretations of this line, of course, but you should see immediately the difference between supporting and not supporting the final word.

Not supporting makes the line a "general" comment—supporting makes it "specific." Remember Stanislavski's famous observation: "In general is the enemy of art."

EXERCISES FOR KICKING THE BOX

Kick the box on the tenth syllable of the blank verse line.

Here are the first four lines of *Sonnet 29*:

When, in disgrace with Fortune and men's eyes,	(1)
I all alone beweep my outcast state,	(2)
And trouble deaf heaven with my bootless cries,	(3)
And look upon myself and curse my fate,	(4)

First, try these two preliminary exercises:

1. Read the four lines, but pay no attention to the final words. Just let that final word of each sentence fall away, as we do in everyday speech.
2. Then read the four lines as if you've run out of breath before reaching the end of each line.

Having done that, put your cardboard box (size doesn't matter) in the middle of the room, and read the four lines again. This time, kick the box on the words "eyes," "state," "cries," and "fate." To do this successfully, you must prepare your body and your kicking leg in the space before the final word in each line; you must position yourself. If you don't prepare, you'll kick too soon or too late. So practice this until you have it perfectly. The box will be a mess, and you'll probably need a new one. (So that the lines make sense, don't forget to use the caesuras—probably after "Fortune," "alone," "heaven," and "myself.")

When doing the exercise correctly, you will notice many things. By "playing" the final word of each line, the line takes on new meaning. Also, the thought in the line is carried through the entire line. The thought then continues on to start the next line.

Because it takes breath support to handle the last word in each line, the air reserve held for that word actually helps support the *entire* line, which provides a double benefit.

When you support the final words, you will notice your diaphragm tighten, and the tension will feel a little uncomfortable. A more "natural" feeling would be to let these final words slide away gently and not to tighten the diaphragm. But that manner of speaking ignores correct vocal support.

When you kick the box on the last word of each line, notice how your entire body gets involved in the language. You want to breathe, and *can* breathe, after you kick—unless there is no punctuation. That breath helps you prepare for the next line. As you get better at this exercise, you'll discover that as you breathe *in,* your mind is grabbing the next line. As you breathe *out,* that next line is spoken. The procedure keeps repeating.

To check how much better the lines are now, read them again and let the last words fade away. Don't kick the box. Compare!

So pause awhile . . .

Practice this exercise with your monologue and sonnet. If you encounter a final word of many syllables, be disciplined. Kick only on the final syllable—not at the start of the word.

Here are the next two lines from *Sonnet 29.* Notice the final word in line 6:

Wishing me like to one more rich in hope, *(kick on "hope")* (5)
Featured like him, like him with friends possessed, *(kick on "sessed")* (6)

You will also find that you can kick the box on any word that is followed by punctuation. For example, in line 6 above, you could also kick on the first "him." Normally we don't play pronouns. In this case we might elect to give it a modest stress. (Use the caesura—probably after "one.")

When the final phrase or word of a line is supported, the thought doesn't "end" until another person speaks. Even when a speech contains a period or semi-colon, continued support of the final word in each line keeps the listeners attentive—they know you have more to say.

I trust I may have leave to speak,
And speak I will.
THE TAMING OF THE SHREW, IV, iii

When you allow the final word of the line to sag, it sounds like you've finished speaking. An imaginary "period" is heard. Then, if you begin talking again, the listener, who thought you had finished, must adjust. Nothing is keeping the thought going. You don't want that situation. You don't want the listener to "relax," but to stay attentive to what you are saying. Don't let 'em off the hook!

We don't want to abuse this exercise and overdo stress on the final syllable or word. Let your common sense and good ear be your judge. The intention is to support, not blast, and allow the idea to continue.

Supporting the final words keeps the listener hooked.

> *I bring a trumpet to awake his ear,*
> *To set his seat on the attentive bent,*
> *And then to speak.*
> TROILUS AND CRESSIDA, I, iii

So pause awhile . . .

MORE VALUES FROM KICKING THE BOX

Is it even so? Begin you to grow upon me?
AS YOU LIKE IT, I, i

Playing the final word of the line will help continue the thought to the next line.

From *The Merchant of Venice*, here is the first line of Portia's well-known "mercy" speech:

Portia: The quality of mercy is not strained;   (IV, i.)

What's the line about? It is not simply about this thing called the "quality of mercy," but suggests that mercy cannot be obtained by *straining* at it.

(Where does the caesura go? Probably after "mercy.")

Read the line aloud and let "is not strained" drop away. Notice that the line seemed to be about "the quality of mercy" and something else, which was rather vague. It was vague for two reasons:
- It was hard to hear
- The actor gave it no importance, so why should I, the listener, spend time with it?

As the next line is already coming to my ear, I have no time to deal with the "unimportant" phrase.

Now, read the line and play the condition of that quality called mercy—in other words, play the final three words of the line. Do this aloud. Voilà! Now the line is about something specific, namely that we don't achieve the quality called mercy by straining at it. And that is the thought in the line. If you don't play the entire line, you leave out the thought.

If your Portia allows me, the listener, to hear only "the quality of mercy (something)," I may continue listening, probably passively, but I'm not encouraged and challenged to do so. And what your character is saying seems loosely defined, not specific. On the other hand, if your Portia tells me that this "thing called mercy isn't obtained by straining," my mind jumps to the possibilities of that idea, and I want to hear what else you have to say—I want to hear the reasoning that supports your statement. Now, you've got me hooked actively, not passively. I want to hear the next line.

Here's the opening line to the same play:

Antonio: In sooth I know not why I am so sad.   (i, i.)

Say the line aloud and allow "so sad" to fall away. What's the line about? It seems to be about something called "sooth" and "why" of something, or "not why" about whatever. Now, say the line aloud and play "so sad." What's the line about? (Caesura? Try it after "sooth" or "why.")

Here's a famous line:

Hamlet: To be, or not to be—that is the question: (*Ham*, iii, i.)

Do the same exercise, first allowing "the question" to fall away. Define what the line is about. Then play "the question" and define what the line is about.

(Punctuation breaks up the phrases, so no caesura is needed.)

Together with supporting the final word of each line, you must also think about supporting *the entire final phrase of each line*. Here is the beginning of *Sonnet 92*:

> But do thy worst to steal thyself away,
> For term of life thou art assured mine;

Do the same exercise, speaking the two lines aloud and allowing "to steal thyself away" and "thou art assured mine" to fade out. (Be sure to make three syllables of "as-sur-`ed.") What are the lines about? Probably "worst" and "life."

Now, play the ending phrases and don't forget to kick the box on the final word of each line. (Don't forget to use the caesura—probably after "worst" and "life.") What are the lines about? Now we're dealing with someone wanting out (perhaps of a relationship) and the speaker asserting that this someone is, in the speaker's view, emotionally owned by him/her.

The study of analysis could be started here, and you can already see the marvelous opportunities for brain work with just these two lines. What are all the possibilities of this opening comment? There will be more analysis in chapter 9.

So pause awhile . . .

Now do this exercise aloud with your sonnet and your monologue and have someone check you for:

- Clearly playing the final phrase of each line
- Allowing the thought of the whole line to be released

You've now come miles on the road to playing Shakespeare!

> *To show our simple skill,*
> *That is the true beginning of our end.*
> A MIDSUMMER NIGHT'S DREAM, V, i

SUPPORTING REALISTIC DIALOGUE

Supporting the final word or phrase of the blank verse line is required for sense. This skill will also work with most realistic dialogue. Once you have learned this skill, apply it to all text. When working with prose, including Shakespeare's, you may be amazed to discover how frequently the final word or phrase of the prose line is the most important part. Modern writers are not using blank verse or placing a stress on the tenth syllable, but the idea of supporting the entire second part of the realistic line, if not the last word, will almost always work for you.

Here is Octavius's first speech in George Bernard Shaw's *Man and Superman.* Observe the final word and phrase of each line.

Octavious: But he had daughters; and yet he was as good to my sister as to
me. And his death was so sudden! I always intended to thank

him—to let him know that I had not taken all his care of me as a matter of course, as any boy takes his father's care. But I waited for an opportunity; and now he is dead—dropped without a moment's warning. He will never know what I felt.   (I, i.)

Here is the opening speech of Arthur Miller's *A View From the Bridge*, spoken by the lawyer, Alfieri:

Alfieri: You wouldn't have known it, but something amusing has just happened. You see how uneasily they nod to me? That's because I am a lawyer. In this neighborhood to meet a lawyer or a priest on the street is unlucky. We're only thought of in connection with disasters, and they'd rather not get too close.   (I, i.)

Except for the second sentence, note how supporting final words and phrases will work with this speech. As for the second sentence, we rarely want to emphasize pronouns or put a question mark on a question. Playing "me" would be wrong for both reasons. Supporting the phrase, "they nod to me," however, would be correct.

Here are two examples of Shakespeare's prose. First, the Duke in *Measure for Measure*:

Duke: The hand that hath made you fair hath made you good. The goodness that is cheap in beauty makes beauty brief in goodness; but grace, being the soul of your complexion, shall keep the body of it ever fair. The assault that Angelo hath made to you, fortune hath conveyed to my understanding; and, but that frailty hath examples for his falling, I should wonder at Angelo. How will you do to content this substitute, and to save your brother?   (III, i.)

Note how necessary it is to support the final phrase of each line, and how sometimes the final word also needs special attention.

Here is Sir Toby Belch in *Twelfth Night*:

Toby: Go, Sir Andrew. Scout me for him at the corner of the orchard like a bum-baily. So soon as ever thou seest him, draw; and as thou draw'st, swear horrible; for it comes to pass oft that a terrible oath, with a swaggering accent sharply twanged off, gives manhood more approbation than ever proof itself would have earned him. Away!   (III, iv.)

Notice how the final word in the internal phrases and in the first complete sentence carries great importance. You would want to stress "bumbaily," "draw," both "swear" and "horrible," and, in the second complete sentence, the final phrase "that ever proof itself would have earned him." Of course, you would not stress "him." Stress pronouns only by specific choice and only when needed for the sense, which is seldom.

Most writers have their own style for dialogue, and some may intentionally "fade out" lines, like songs that don't know how to end. But you can't go wrong by keeping the idea of "kicking the box" close at hand. Test all of your realistic dialogue with this skill. Not only will the skill help you to sustain the thoughts, it will give you insight into the various meanings of the lines and teach you when to breathe.

See how apt it is to learn
Any hard lesson that may do thee good.
MUCH ADO ABOUT NOTHING, I, i

USEFUL IDEAS TO REMEMBER:

CHAPTER 5

Practice the Breathing Skill

A SIMPLE TECHNIQUE to practice is this: Breathe at the natural stops, which are identified by punctuation marks. We could argue that the punctuation may be corrupt, so why follow it?

Pick any modern edition of Shakespeare (we're using *The Pelican Shakespeare*), and you have the punctuation that has evolved over four hundred years, often suggested by the world's most brilliant literary minds. That's a pretty good starting place.

Then trust your ear. If the punctuation seems wrong and your ear tells you it should be elsewhere, move it accordingly. The actor is ultimately in charge of the language and must speak with confidence.

YOU'VE GOT TO BREATHE!

Assuming the punctuation in our selected edition is acceptable, note what happens if you breathe "at random." Here are the first four lines of *Sonnet 143*:

> Lo, as a careful housewife runs to catch
> One of her feathered creatures broke away,
> Sets down her babe, and makes all swift dispatch
> In pursuit of the thing she would have stay;

If you breathe after "catch" simply because you're out of breath or because on paper it looks like the end of the line, the first two lines won't make sense. Try it, and you'll see that the first line "ends" if you breathe after "catch," and that it is not a complete sentence. This reading would jar the listener's ear. The second line becomes the beginning of a speech, ignoring the incomplete first line, and messes up the third line. Lines 1 and 3 are typical enjambed lines, because the thought continues without punctuation. The actor must play the thought, and breathe only when it is completed. Sometimes you can play two or more thoughts on one breath, but you should avoid breaking a single thought into more than one breath.

Tyrone Guthrie liked to say that any well-trained actor could speak seven lines of blank verse on one breath, in a large theatre, with clear diction and without rushing. (*On Acting*, 14) If you can't do that now, it's a good exercise to work on.

Read the first two lines in one breath (you can breathe after "Lo," if you wish), and note the sense. If you play "catch" (but don't breathe after it) and play "away," (and do breathe after it) the speech keeps moving forward—we know there is more to come.

(Don't forget to use the caesura—probably after "housewife," "creatures," and "thing.")

Here are the first two lines of *Sonnet 15*:

> When I consider everything that grows
> Holds in perfection but a little moment,

Again, don't breathe after "grows," although it might be followed by a caesura, because you need to set up "Holds" in the second line for sense.

The second line is not a "regular" blank verse line, because there is a stress on the first syllable, "Holds." How do we know that? Your common sense tells you that the verb "Holds" must be played, and that it would be silly to read the line with "Holds" unstressed and "in" stressed. Try it and you'll see. This line is an example of Shakespeare breaking the rhythm for effect.

Try the two lines taking a caesura after "grows" (but not a breath). Try it without the caesura. Trying to say "grows Holds" together isn't comfortable. It also destroys the active verb "Holds." Caesuras are often taken at special places, where we might need a little pause to point up a word or thought, but don't need a breath. (Caesuras might be inserted after "consider" and "perfection," plus the extra caesura needed after "grows.")

Look at these lines in which Macbeth decides to kill Banquo and Fleance:

Macbeth:	To be thus is nothing, but to be safely thus—	(1)
	Our fears in Banquo stick deep,	(2)
	And in his royalty of nature reigns that	(3)
	Which would be feared. 'Tis much he dares;	(4)
	And to that dauntless temper of his mind	(5)
	He hath a wisdom that doth guide his valour	(6)
	To act in safety. There is none but he	(7)
	Whose being I do fear; and under him	(8)
	My genius is rebuked, as it is said	(9)
	Mark Antony's was by Caesar.	(*Mac*, III, i.) (10)

This speech contains typical Shakespearean punctuation, as clearly as we can tell. We must remember that our versions of the plays were taken from actors' scripts. Different editions of the plays change the punctuation slightly.

So pause awhile …

The breathing points are the punctuation marks. Circle them, then read the speech and breathe at each mark. You will find that it is quite easy to speak from one breathing point to the next. The longest stretch is two and one-half lines.

Don't breathe after "Banquo" in line 2 or "nature" in line 3. But try it once to discover the problem. You will see immediately that the choice is wrong. Your common sense and good ear will tell you.

Don't breathe at the end of a verse line simply because it is the end of the line on paper. Unless there is punctuation, the end of the line isn't the end of the phrase or thought. Breathe at the end of the verse line only if there is punctuation.

So pause awhile …

Read these four lines, which have numerous punctuation points, and breathe at each natural stop (all of the punctuation points). Ariel, a spirit, greets his master, Prospero, who has sent for him, in *The Tempest*.

Ariel:	All hail, great master! Grave sir, hail! I come	(1)
	To answer thy best pleasure; be 't to fly,	(2)
	To swim, to dive into the fire, to ride	(3)

On the curled clouds. To thy strong bidding task   (4)
Ariel and all his quality.   (I, ii.) (5)

Did you cheat? *Read it a second time and make yourself breathe at all punctuation points.* You will notice that you don't need that many breaths. You may be able to read the first line breathing only after "master" and the second "hail," thereby cutting two breaths. But don't cut them unless you don't need them. You probably would have used the breaths in the three-thousand seat original Globe Theatre, but won't use them in most modern theatres or for film. If you use breaths after "fly," "swim," and "fire," they may help you create images with each phrase, which may be appropriate for the character.

Trust your judgment. Your goal is to have a reserve of breath power available at all times and to be able to kick the box on the final word of a sentence. If you haven't enough breath to support the final word, you are not breathing correctly. Inserting more breaths into the lines is not the best solution (although it is one), because these added breaths break up the thought in the verse line in an unnatural way and may leave you gasping and unclear. If you need to insert a breath, do it where the phrasing allows and where it will add emphasis to what you just said or are about to say.

Your goal is to breathe correctly—to fill your lungs at each breathing point—and to avoid little gasping breaths that fill only one-third of your lung capacity. Take the time to breathe deeply, and then speak the line on the exhale. The words ride on air; just send them out.

> *Yet words do well*
> *When he that speaks them pleases those that hear.*
> AS YOU LIKE IT, III, V

Actors accustomed to realistic text often want to "enhance" that text with sounds, gasps, crying, whispering, pauses for effect, sighs, and "ahs." With heightened text, "enhancements" tend to destroy the rhythm of the line. When the rhythm is lost, the antithetical ideas and images are lost, and the audience listens only passively because they are not quite certain what you are saying.

For an excellent example of reading heightened text with great heart and commitment, correct breathing, and without breaking the rhythm with unnecessary pauses or character "enhancements," watch Kenneth Branagh speak the Saint Crispin's speech in Act IV of his film, *Henry V.* It's perfection. Other similar examples are listed in part 4.

Embellishing the language with emotion because "my character would do this" will usually not work for you in Shakespeare. Your performance becomes indulgent, because you've lost *what* is being said in favor of *how* it is being said. Generally this direction works: If you need to cry, cry after the line, not on the line. Reason? We must hear the words first, then we can experience your sorrow without the irritation caused by a muffled and unclear line.

If you must whisper, and risk the irritation caused by the muffled line, do it so that everyone, including the back row, can hear and understand clearly. You can even rant and rave with a powerful voice and great energy, and the audience will listen only passively if they don't know exactly what you are saying.

So pause awhile ...

Here is a good rehearsal exercise. Clearly mark the breathing points in your monologue. Then read the speech aloud, and use up all of your air on each group of words from breathing point to breathing point—one breath, one thought. Make certain that you support the final words, but otherwise, empty your lungs between breathing points.

With this exercise, you will discover how much force and power you have available. It also implants in your mind the necessity to breathe. Use all of the air between breathing points, even if the line has only one word.

As you practice this exercise, you will begin to notice that taking the breath gives you the split second you need to grasp your next line. As you inhale physically, you also inhale mentally, so to speak, and grab the next line. Then out it comes on the next breath.

If it is your tendency as an actor to break up lines with "embellishments" for emotional effect, the above exercise may convince you that the only pauses you really need in Shakespeare are the breathing points. Keep the pauses intact, the words moving, and play the antithetical ideas against each other. You will discover that the application of too much emotion to heightened text does nothing but bury the meaning, so the audience stops listening.

As with all good acting, don't get ahead of yourself by thinking ahead. Stay in the moment, listen, respond. Don't anticipate or indicate. Realize that after you speak a line, your breathing skill allows you to mentally secure your next line, and this skill will help you develop the confidence to stay in the moment.

If you have three or four lines with no breathing points, try to conquer them. You will need a deep breath before you start line 1 and will need to control the release of your air, or you'll never make it through and surely won't have anything left for the important final word.

So pause awhile . . .

Try this example, as the Bishop of Canterbury tells King Henry V that, if he will attack France, the Church will supply him with the money needed for the campaign.

Canterbury:	O, let their bodies follow, my dear liege,	(1)
	With blood, and sword, and fire to win your right!	(2)
	In aid whereof we of the spiritualty	(3)
	Will raise your highness such a mighty sum	(4)
	As never did the clergy at one time	(5)
	Bring in to any of your ancestors. (*HV*, i, ii.)	(6)

Read the speech aloud and see if you can do lines 3–6 without a breath. If you can't make it, take a breath after "sum," but notice that the speech flows better without the breath. Note, too, that "spiritualty" must be elided to three syllables.

Try these lines of Chorus before Act IV in *Henry V.*

Chorus:	Now entertain conjecture of a time	(1)
	When creeping murmur and the poring dark	(2)
	Fills the wide vessel of the universe.	(3)
	From camp to camp, through the foul womb of night,	(4)
	The hum of either army stilly sounds,	(5)
	That the fixed sentinels almost receive	(6)
	The secret whispers of each other's watch. (iv, Cho.)	(7)

Read the speech aloud, breathing only at the punctuation. Support all last words, especially "universe," "sounds," and "watch." Don't insert a breath after "dark."

Keep these simple clues in mind:
- The words ride out on the breath; just send them.
- Inhaling gives you a moment to grasp your next line.
- Breathe at every opportunity. If you cut a breathing point, do it intentionally because you don't need it.
- Strong breathing gives you power; lack of breath signals weakness.

Always read and work on Shakespeare aloud. This language is meant to be spoken, and much of the sense is discovered through speech. Shakespeare doesn't just work better aloud, it works *ten times better*! Therefore, when you work on the lines, use the opportunity to practice breathing and voice skills as well.

Once you can use these basic tools, you've come even farther on the journey to playing Shakespeare.

> *Ay, marry, sir, now it begins to work.*
> THE TAMING OF THE SHREW, III, ii

USEFUL IDEAS TO REMEMBER:

CHAPTER 6

Practice the Speaking Skill

Now mark him, he begins again to speak.
JULIUS CAESAR, III, ii

M ODERN ACTOR TRAINING in America emphasizes memory recall, playing the subtext, and character development. In many ways, this training makes words secondary to feelings. The actor nowadays tends to "reflect" on the thought, then express it by "handling" the words. The actor may manipulate the words to express the subtextual thought.

The moment required to reflect creates a pause. That "pause to reflect" may come at anytime—before the thought, in midthought, or after the thought. The placement and length of the various pauses are based on how the character *feels* about the thought. During a "pause to reflect," the actor usually breathes and reflects, which makes it a different kind of pause than the no-breath caesura—which is a pause to *set up* a word or thought and is not intended to provide time to "reflect."

Today, this pause-to-reflect acting style dominates most films, stage productions of many realistic plays, and especially modern scripts, which call for great subtextual clarification. This technique is at the core of realistic acting.

A problem with this approach emerges, however, when the more important requirement of "playing your action" becomes secondary to "playing your feeling." Because the desire to play your feeling is so grounded in realistic actor training, even good actors often forget to play their action first.

When an actor allows the concept of "playing your feeling" to dominate, the end result is often indulgent acting. The result of indulgent acting is ponderous text, unrealized author intentions, and loss of audience.

SAY WHAT YOU THINK WHEN YOU THINK IT

With Shakespeare, you will be most successful if you
- Say what you think when you think it while . . .
- Playing your action

By "say what you think," I mean, cut out the moment of "reflection" on the thought and simply speak the thought. Don't think, then talk. Just think while you talk. In other words, act *on* the words, not *between* them.

Shakespeare's language is written so that the actor rarely needs to "reflect" to express feelings or reasoning, because characters say aloud what they are reasoning and feeling. In Shakespeare, the thought is not hidden in the subtext. What's to be said is right there on the surface.

For many actors, dealing with this concept is not easy. The dominance of subtextual acting in film is embedded in our minds. We hear most dialogue read with pauses and searching and poured-out feelings. If we've never tackled Shakespeare before, it is possible that all of our acting has been based on subtextual line readings.

Yet, to determine that language written hundreds of years ago might require different speaking skills than modern language is not really surprising. After all, if a good play, as Hamlet says, intends "to hold, as 'twere, the mirror up to nature," then both modern and Elizabethan writers will mirror their respective languages and speaking habits.

When Shakespeare's language was written, the concepts of "character" and "subtext" as we think of them today were unknown. In the sixteenth and seventeenth centuries, before Sigmund Freud and electronic media, people probably spoke feelings and thoughts more clearly than we do today. Writings of the period demonstrate that practice. In modern-day conversation, however, our tendency is often to disguise what we mean. We are taught as children to "be polite" and not to annoy others with what we really think or feel.

As the thought in modern plays is revealed more in the subtext (what you're thinking) than in the text (what you're saying), modern acting focuses on the skills required to find and speak that subtext. But Shakespeare didn't write that way.

As you study *what* and *why* a specific Shakespearean character is speaking, you will discover that the words are exactly the same as the thoughts.

The character is saying exactly what he or she means. So you don't need to play the subtext. In fact, your work will be stronger if you forget acting subtext and, in doing so, remove the "reflective" pauses.

Certainly there are subtextual thoughts in Shakespeare. The point is that the thoughts are also in the language. If useful, of course, and if you are playing the language convincingly, you can work with whatever subtext seems necessary. But in doing so remember that Shakespeare put the thought into the spoken words. Your "subtext" will be a modern-day application; it may cause you to lose the rhythm, and your acting may become indulgent, ponderous, and unclear.

> *Answer every man directly.—Ay, and briefly.—Ay, and wisely.*
> JULIUS CAESAR, III, iii

WORKING WITH SUBTEXT

Here are some examples of speeches that could be broken up for subtextual reflection—so the character can "feel it"—or could be spoken *without* the reflection, in which case the character, without taking pause, says directly what he or she is thinking or feeling. See which way works better for you.

In *The Merchant of Venice*, Antonio is about to lose "a pound of flesh," and probably his life, to Shylock. Bassanio, who created the problem, has this to say:

Bassanio: Antonio, I am married to a wife
　　　　　 Which is as dear to me as life itself;
　　　　　 But life itself, my wife, and all the world
　　　　　 Are not with me esteemed above thy life.
　　　　　 I would lose all, ay, sacrifice them all
　　　　　 Here to this devil, to deliver you.　　　　　　　　(IV, i.)

Read the speech through a couple of times for sense. Next, let's create some subtext. Be Bassanio and read the speech, playing these basic feelings about the situation. Play out each one.

1. Hate Shylock: Create a subtext which says, "I hate this man," and play the speech around that subtext.
2. Love your wife: Create a subtext around your great love for Portia and how tragic it would be to lose her.
3. Persuade Antonio of your love: Create a subtext that allows you to thoroughly assure Antonio that you would do anything for him.

4. Apologize: Create a subtext that says how sorry you are to have allowed this problem to develop.

Here are possible results of these four subtextual readings:
1. With this subtext, the speech is about your hatred of Shylock.
2. With this subtext, the speech is about *your* sacrifice, not Antonio's.
3. With this subtext, the speech is about the struggle within *you*, not what Antonio is facing.
4. With this subtext, the speech turns sentimental and indulgent.

Now just read the speech as it is written, adding nothing, but taking this moment to reaffirm your honest feelings to Antonio. Say what you think as you think it. Your action, "to reaffirm," is measured in Antonio and how he responds to you.

Isn't everything you need right there in the words? Is it necessary to apply subtext? Is it necessary to be extremely emotional for any reason? Is it necessary to take any pauses other than the natural breathing points?

Also notice that when playing any of the four subtext examples, you forget to *play your action*. You lose sight of your objective, because your concentration is on a subtextual *feeling*. The action is lost, because those feelings, when expressed, are all descriptive.

To hear and see some other examples, in part 4 are listed a few film and video performances that may be helpful. I've indicated in what way the various performances are successful. Some are brilliant, and these clearly illustrate the points we're discussing.

ACHIEVE YOUR OBJECTIVE

In *The Comedy of Errors*, Antipholus of Ephesus tries to inform the Duke about the ill treatment to which he has been subjected by his wife and others.

Ant/Eph: By the way we met
My wife, her sister, and a rabble more
Of vile confederates. Along with them
They brought one Pinch, a hungry lean-faced villain,
A mere anatomy, a mountebank,
A threadbare juggler, and a fortune-teller,
A needy, hollow-eyed, sharp-looking wretch,
A living dead man. This pernicious slave,
Forsooth, took on him as a conjurer,

And gazing in mine eyes, feeling my pulse,
And with no face, as 'twere, out-facing me,
Cries out, I was possessed. Then all together
They fell upon me, bound me, bore me thence,
And in a dark and dankish vault at home
There left me and my man, both bound together,
Till, gnawing with my teeth my bonds in sunder,
I gained my freedom, and immediately
Ran hither to your Grace; whom I beseech
To give me ample satisfaction
For these deep shames and great indignities. (v, i.)

Read the speech through a couple of times for sense. Next, be Antipholus and apply the following subtextual possibilities.

1. Get vengeance: Convince the Duke how evil was this fellow, Pinch, and carefully describe all his characteristics.
2. Hate your wife: Create a subtext which places all blame on her.
3. Despise what happened to you: Create a subtext which allows you to feel sorry for yourself.
4. Seek sympathy: Create a subtext which draws sympathy from the Duke.

Here are possible results of these four subtextual readings:

1. In this reading, you completely lose track of your objective—which is not about Pinch.
2. In this reading, "he doth protest too much!"
3. In this reading, the action you are playing to achieve your objective is colored with whining and whimpering, and I soon lose interest.
4. In this reading, you are trying to guide the Duke's feelings, therefore playing the wrong action, which is to seek his reasoned justice, to which you are entitled.

Use the language to achieve your objective. Now you are Antipholus, so say what you think as you think it and reach for your objective. Know each action, and state clearly and emphatically what happened to you.

Don't dwell on Pinch, but use your memory of him to accent how you were treated, and move the entire first part of the speech to reach the line, "I was possessed." (That is your "proof" that your accusers are liars.) Your action is to reduce your accusers to liars—so reduce them.

Now, play the second part of the speech to reach the line "and great indignities." Notice, there are no full stops between "Then all together" and "great indignities." As quickly as you relate one thing, the next thing is on your lips. There is a great urgency to reach "give me ample satisfaction," and then the final line, which summarizes why you deserve that satisfaction.

Your objective is to obtain satisfaction—so obtain it. "Detours" from this action are not required. Your success is measured in what the Duke does when you finish.

Here are additional notes for working on this speech. If you set out to obtain satisfaction, you won't delay unnecessarily to describe Pinch, to seek sympathy, or for any other reason. If you select too much indignation, we lose interest; too much excitement and we lose the reasoning; too much anger and the emotion buries the words—and we don't hear your argument. Find the balance between your built-up frustration over what happened to you and your need to obtain satisfaction.

If you appear to be "mad," your accusers will appear to be right. You must use your reason to (1) prove your sanity by control of your actions, and (2) prove you are deserving of satisfaction. Balance your reason and your emotion to achieve your objective and allow your argument to be heard. Reach for your objective, and the action will pull you along without delay.

He has strangled
His language in his tears.
HENRY VIII, V, i

———

I speak as my understanding instructs me . . .
THE WINTER'S TALE, I, i

———

USEFUL IDEAS TO REMEMBER:

CHAPTER 7

Working with Structure and Rhythm

REFER TO THE SONNET you have selected. To understand speech structure is only one of many reasons why you should work on sonnets. Notice how the sonnet develops. In fourteen lines, there is usually an opening statement or idea, followed by development of the idea, and a concluding thought. In the sonnet, the concluding thought is expressed in a rhyming couplet.

The *basic line structure* through which the thought is expressed is usually 4-4-4-2. Some sonnets do not have a full stop (i.e., period, question mark, exclamation point) until the end of the final line, and the main thought is carried for fourteen lines. Others have full stops after each four lines. The structure is determined by the way Shakespeare chooses to develop the thought.

SPEECH STRUCTURE

I pray, can you read anything you see?
Ay, if I know the letters and language.
ROMEO AND JULIET, I, ii

Shakespeare's speeches are structured much the same as sonnets. There is usually an idea stated and then developed, followed by a concluding or summary thought.

Since most speeches are in three parts, the actor can use the structure as a guide to performance choices.

The opening idea needs to be clearly stated, or the development will fall on deaf ears. The development section often includes the rich poetry, the imagery, and the antithetical thoughts, and can be the hardest part of the speech to make clear. Handle the conclusion with conviction.

The speech structure is such that one can cut a Shakespearean play to less than one hour by simply keeping the opening and closing of each speech and taking out the poetry, which is usually in the middle. What you have left is the action line without the richness.

So pause awhile . . .

Using your rehearsal material, break up the sonnet and the monologue so that you isolate the opening thought, the development, and the conclusion. Check your work against these two examples.

Here are a sonnet and a monologue, which will illustrate and compare speech structure. First the sonnet:

Sonnet 57

Being your slave, what should I do but tend	(1)
Upon the hours and times of your desire?	(2)
I have no precious time at all to spend,	(3)
Nor services to do, till you require.	(4)
Nor dare I chide the world-without-end hour	(5)
Whilst I, my sovereign, watch the clock for you,	(6)
Nor think the bitterness of absence sour	(7)
When you have bid your servant once adieu;	(8)
Nor dare I question with my jealous thought	(9)
Where you may be, or your affairs suppose,	(10)
But, like a sad slave, stay and think of nought	(11)
Save, where you are how happy you make those.	(12)
So true a fool is love that in your will,	(13)
Though you do any thing, he thinks no ill.	(14)

Lines 1 and 2 set out the thought and end with a full stop.

Lines 3 and 4 explain the thought. Then there is another full stop.

Lines 5–8 explore the thought; there is no full stop, and the exploration continues.

Lines 9–12 take the idea even farther, and end with a full stop.

Lines 13 and 14 summarize the reason for the problem that was pondered in the previous ten lines, after being set out in the first two.

A BRIEF DIVERSION

If you wish to work on this sonnet, here are some ideas. Don't get all sentimental. Instead, play the irony. Play the tongue in cheek, laughing at yourself for having gotten so deeply into this love affair that you excuse whatever your lover does.

There are other ways to read these lines, but this approach introduces you to the irony playable in the sonnets and cautions against sarcasm or sentimentality.

Sarcasm is always the *last* choice you should make for a line reading. Use it only if the character choice absolutely demands that the thought intended for the listener is sarcastic.

Oh, horrors! When we think back on the sarcastic acting style of the film industry of the 1930s through the 1950s, or if we listen to many modern soap operas or turn on prime time television or watch (and hear) any number of film stars read every line with sarcasm, we ask, "How did that happen to American realistic acting?" It surely wasn't Stanislavski's intention!"

> *Who has read or heard*
> *Of any kindred action like to this?*
> KING JOHN, III, iv

Here is an example of speech structure in a monologue. Claudius, King of Denmark, speaks to Hamlet's friends Rosencrantz and Guildenstern.

King:	Welcome, dear Rosencrantz and Guildenstern.	(1)
	Moreover that we much did long to see you,	(2)
	The need we have to use you did provoke	(3)
	Our hasty sending. Something have you heard	(4)
	Of Hamlet's transformation—so call it,	(5)
	Sith nor th' exterior nor the inward man	(6)
	Resembles that it was. What it should be,	(7)
	More than his father's death, that thus hath put him	(8)
	So much from th' understanding of himself,	(9)
	I cannot dream of: I entreat you both	(10)
	That, being of so young days brought up with him,	(11)
	And sith so neighbored to his youth and havior,	(12)

That you vouchsafe your rest here in our court	(13)
Some little time, so by your companies	(14)
To draw him on to pleasures, and to gather	(15)
So much as from occasion you may glean,	(16)
Whether aught to us unknown afflicts him thus,	(17)
That opened lies within our remedy. *(Ham,* 11, ii.)	(18)

Line 1 is a standard greeting.

Lines 2, 3, and part of 4 point out that "we have a need" and a problem.

Lines 4 through part of 10 review the problem.

Lines 10 through part of 14 are an invitation.

Lines 14–18 are the command to Rosencrantz and Guildenstern to get to the bottom of the problem.

Speech structure may vary, depending on length and intention, but an awareness of the basic form will serve you well. In Shakespeare's speeches, you can usually ask the following questions and find answers:

- What is the speech about (or what is the thought)?
- What is the development?
- What is the conclusion?

Use your awareness of this structure to play your action and achieve your objective.

BREAKING THE RHYTHM

How "meter" differs from "rhythm" can be confusing for some actors.

Technically, meter is the measured arrangement of words into a specific pattern, which is, for us, lines of five feet (each a meter), with each foot comprised of two syllables.

Rhythm is (for us) the recurring pattern of strong and weak accents within the meter (the foot). Thus, here are five meters with recurring rhythm:

dee dum / dee dum / dee dum / dee dum / dee dum.

This explanation seems to work for actors: Meter is the written structure, rhythm is what we hear.

Of the many marvelous things about Shakespeare's language, one of the most unique is the effect achieved when he breaks the rhythm. As an actor, you've got to know when this change is happening, and you must play it accordingly. If you don't do so, the complete sense of the line is lost.

For example, notice the break in this rhythm:

dee dum / dee dum / dum dee / dee dum / dee dum.

There are hundreds of examples of breaking the rhythm, and once your eye (and ear) are searching, you'll soon identify them. Here are a few. From *Henry VI, Part 2*:

York:	How now? Is Somerset at liberty?	(1)
	Then, York, unloose thy long-imprisoned thoughts	(2)
	And let thy tongue be equal with thy heart.	(3)
	Shall I endure the sight of Somerset?	(4)
	False king, why hast thou broken faith with me,	(5)
	Knowing how hardly I can brook abuse?	(6)
	King did I call thee? No! thou art not king,	(7)
	Not fit to govern and rule multitudes,	(8)
	Which dar'st not, no, nor canst not rule a traitor.	(v, i.) (9)

The meter is broken to start lines 6 and 7, so the rhythm changes in each of these first feet to "dum dee." As an actor choice, in lines 4 and 5 you could argue that the rhythm of the first foot in each line would be "dum dum," with no unstressed syllable. In line 7, you could argue that every word is stressed. (In monosyllabic lines like this, watch for many stresses!) Know the possibilities, and make your personal choice.

From *Richard III*, Clarence speaks to his murderers:

Clarence:	I charge you, as you hope to have redemption	(1)
	By Christ's dear blood shed for our grievous sins,	(2)
	That you depart, and lay no hands on me:	(3)
	The deed you undertake is damnable.	(i, iv.) (4)

The meter is broken in line 2 by "shed," which is an active verb that must be stressed, but is in the unstressed position. You need the verb, and certainly "for" (the other half of the foot) would not be the stressed syllable. So a caesura is taken after "blood" to set up "shed," which is stressed. (As an actor choice, once you stress "shed" you could also stress "for" to achieve a specific emphasis.)

The other three lines are regular, with line 1 having a feminine ending. From *The Comedy of Errors*:

Duke:	One of these men is genius to the other;	(1)
	And so of these, which is the natural man,	(2)
	And which the spirit? Who deciphers them?	(3)

Dromio S: I, sir, am Dromio; command him away.   (4)
Dromio E: I, sir, am Dromio; pray, let me stay.   (v, i.) (5)

In line 2, "which" breaks the meter. In the Dromio lines, both "I's" break the meter.

So pause awhile ...

Scan your rehearsal monologue and sonnet for words that break the meter. Circle them. These are obviously important words and must be played. They are real clues to reading the lines.

> *Scan this thing no further; leave it to time.*
> OTHELLO, III, iii

USEFUL IDEAS TO REMEMBER:

CHAPTER 8

Practice Identifying Antithesis

Iₙ ᴛʜᴇ sᴛᴜᴅʏ of how Shakespeare's language works, nothing is more important than understanding antithesis. According to Webster, "Antithesis is the placing of a sentence or one of its parts against another to which it is opposed to form a balanced contrast of ideas."

For text awareness, you should not rely on your director. First, textual study is part of the actor's job; to know exactly what you are saying is part of the work. Secondly, American directors are often more interested in the visual element of a production than the textual. That approach, if not balanced with the time needed to thoroughly analyze the text, can spell disaster for the actors.

If you are working in a situation where the text is not being studied for antithetical words, phrases and thoughts, you need to work especially hard on your own. You might also seek private coaching or assemble a group of actors outside rehearsal and do this work. Without text study, your acting will fall short of your capability.

For the actor, discovering antithesis is both enriching and exciting. Discovery is not an academic exercise. Rather, it turns on the brain, and does so in such a way that it fuels emotion and spontaneity. Text study gives you confidence; it does not take away confidence. (That very thought is antithetical!)

Shakespeare read without playing the antithesis sounds generalized, and we all know what Stanislavski said about "in general." On the other hand, when you *play* the antithetical words, phrases, and thoughts, the meaning becomes specific.

Because you want your acting to be specific, seek opportunities for text study. Realize that each antithetical idea you dig out and play will make your acting stronger.

So pause awhile . . .

ANTITHESIS: THE ACTOR'S FRIEND

Here are exercises in locating antithesis. In the first examples, the antithetical ideas are identified. Then there are examples to practice on your own.

For this second group of examples, the answers are hidden in the next two chapters. After digging out the antithetical ideas as best you can, turn to that help and compare. You may even find more examples than are identified. Also, for this work, five or six brains are usually better than one, and it's more fun. So get a pizza, put a small group together, and plunge in.

This procedure works well: First, read the speech aloud for general sense, then concentrate on two or four line sections. Read these lines aloud, and dig out the antithetical ideas. After you've finished, read the entire speech aloud, this time playing the discoveries, and listen for *even more* antithesis. For example, the first half of the speech might be antithetical to the second half, or an early line might be antithetical to a later line.

Once you believe that you've exhausted all possibilities, read the speech with the new discoveries, and compare to your first reading.

When in rehearsal, also be aware that any of your speeches may be antithetical to something said by another actor. See, for example, the speeches below.

> *This is all as true as it is strange.*
> *Nay, it is ten times true, for truth is truth*
> *To th'end of reck'ning.*
> MEASURE FOR MEASURE, V, i

Here is Romeo's first speech. He talks of love with his cousin, Benvolio, then notices that a street fight has taken place between the two warring houses.

Benvolio:	Alas, that love, so gentle in his view,	(1)
	Should be so tyrannous and rough in proof!	(2)
Romeo:	Alas, that love, whose view is muffled still,	(3)
	Should without eyes see pathways to his will!	(4)
	Where shall we dine? O me! What fray was here?	(5)
	Yet tell me not, for I have heard it all.	(6)
	Here's much to do with hate, but more with love:	(7)
	Why, then, O brawling love! O loving hate!	(8)
	O any thing, of nothing first create!	(9)
	O heavy lightness! serious vanity!	(10)
	Mis-shapen chaos of well-seeming forms!	(11)
	Feather of lead, bright smoke, cold fire, sick health!	(12)
	Still-waking sleep, that is not what it is!	(13)
	This love feel I, that feel no love in this.	(14)
	Dost thou not laugh?	(15)
Benvolio:	No, cuz, I rather weep. *(Rom, I, i.)*	(16)

Here are some of the antithetical words, phrases, and thoughts. Perhaps you will discover others.

Lines 1/2: The phrases "gentle in his view" and "tyrannous and rough in proof" are antithetical. (The first idea is a pleasant anticipation; the second an unpleasant experience.)

Line 4: "without eyes"—"see pathways"

Line 6: "tell me not"—"have heard it all"

Line 7: "hate"—"love"

Line 8: "brawling"—"love"; "loving"—"hate"

Line 9: "any thing"—"nothing"

Line 10: "heavy"—"lightness"; "serious"—"vanity"

Line 11. "Mis-shapen chaos"—"well-seeming forms"

Line 12: All four phrases.

Line 13: "Still-waking"—"sleep"; "is not"—"is"

Line 14: "love"—"no love"

Lines 15/16: "laugh"—"weep"

Also, the *thought* in line 13—"That's not what it [love] is"—is antithetical to the type of "love" expressed in lines 7–12.

Now read the speech and play all the antithetical possibilities!

In an example from *Henry V*, here is the King's prayer before the battle at Agincourt.

King:	O God of battles, steel my soldiers' hearts;	(1)
	Possess them not with fear! Take from them now	(3)

The sense of reck'ning, if th' opposed numbers (3)
Pluck their hearts from them. Not to-day, O Lord, (4)
O, not to-day, think not upon the fault (5)
My father made in compassing the crown! (6)
I Richard's body have interred new; (7)
And on it have bestowed more contrite tears (8)
Than from it issued forced drops of blood: (9)
Five hundred poor I have in yearly pay, (10)
Who twice a day their withered hands hold up (11)
Toward heaven, to pardon blood; (12)
And I have built two chantries, (13)
Where the sad and solemn priests sing still (14)
For Richard's soul. More will I do: (15)
Though all that I can do is nothing worth, (16)
Since that my penitence comes after all, (17)
Imploring pardon. (IV, i) (18)

Here are some of the antithetical words, phrases, and thoughts.
Lines 1/2: "steel"—"fear"
Lines 3/4: "sense of reck'ning"—"pluck their hearts"
Lines 8/9: "bestow'd"—"issued"; "tears"—"blood"
Line 14: "sad and solemn"—"sing"
Line 16: "all"—"nothing"
Also, the thought—"think not upon the fault"— (lines 5 and 6)—is antithetical to the thought—"think on all of this penitence and award us victory" (lines 7–18).
Here is Olivia encouraging love from Viola in *Twelfth Night:*

Olivia: O, what a deal of scorn looks beautiful (1)
In the contempt and anger of his lip. (2)
A murd'rous guilt shows not itself more soon (3)
Than love that would seem hid: love's night is noon. (4)
Cesario, by the roses of the spring, (5)
By maidhood, honor, truth, and everything, (6)
I love thee so that, maugre all thy pride, (7)
Nor wit nor reason can my passion hide. (8)
Do not extort thy reasons from this clause, (9)
For that I woo, thou therefore hast no cause; (10)
But rather reason thus with reason fetter, (11)
Love sought is good, but given unsought is better. (III, i.) (12)

Clarification note: "maugre" means "despite," and "fetter" is something that confines: (Webster: "boredom puts fetters upon the imagination.")

Antithetical text includes:

Lines 1/2: The idea that scorn, contempt, and anger can be beautiful on the lip is antithetical.

Lines 3/4: "murd'rous guilt"—"love"; "shows"—"hid"; "night"—"noon"

Line 7: The thought "I love thee so" is antithetical to the thought "mauger all thy pride."

Line 8: "wit nor reason"—"passion"

Line 12: "sought"—"unsought"

Also, the thought expressed in lines 1–4—"you hide your love behind scorn and pride"—is antithetical to the thought expressed in lines 5–8—"my love is unhidden and freely expressed."

And in lines 9–12, the thought—"you deny the passion of love"—is antithetical to the thought—"but I'm giving myself to you."

From *Richard III*, here is Queen Margaret (whose husband, King Henry VI, has been killed by Richard) condemning Queen Elizabeth, who succeeded her.

Margaret:	Decline all this, and see what now thou art:	(1)
	For happy wife, a most distressed widow;	(2)
	For joyful mother, one that wails the name;	(3)
	For one being sued to, one that humbly sues;	(4)
	For queen, a very caitiff crowned with care;	(5)
	For she that scorned at me, now scorned of me;	(6)
	For she being feared of all, now fearing one;	(7)
	For she commanding all, obeyed of none.	(8)
	Thus hath the course of justice whirled about	(9)
	And left thee but a very prey to time,	(10)
	Having no more but thought of what thou wast,	(11)
	To torture thee the more, being what thou art. (iv, iv.)	(12)

If you study this entire speech you will discover that these lines, taken from the middle, are antithetical to the lines that preceded them. This speech also contains these antithetical ideas:

Line 1: "Decline"—"now"

Line 2: "happy wife"—"distressed widow"

Line 3: "joyful mother"—"one that wails"

Line 4: "being sued to"—"humbly sues"

Line 5: "queen"—"caitiff"

Line 6: "scorned at me"—"scorned of me"

Line 7: "feared of all"—"fearing one"
Line 8: "commanding all"—"obeyed of none"
Lines 9/10: "course of justice"—"prey to time"
Lines 11/12: "what thou wast"—"what thou art"

So pause awhile . . .

Do these next examples on your own. After finishing, dig around in chapters 9 and 10 and find my listing of the antithetical words, phrases, and thoughts. Perhaps you found more possibilities.

In *The Taming of the Shrew*, here is Petruchio speaking to Kate after he has dismissed the tailors and plans to travel to her father's home in old clothes.

Petruchio:	Well, come, my Kate; we will unto your father's,	(1)
	Even in these honest mean habiliments.	(2)
	Our purses shall be proud, our garments poor,	(3)
	For 'tis the mind that makes the body rich;	(4)
	And as the sun breaks through the darkest clouds	(5)
	So honor peereth in the meanest habit.	(iv, iii.) (6)

In *Richard II*, here is the King alone in prison shortly before his death.

Richard:	I have been studying how I may compare	(1)
	This prison where I live unto the world;	(2)
	And, for because the world is populous,	(3)
	And here is not a creature but myself,	(4)
	I cannot do it. Yet I'll hammer it out.	(5)
	My brain I'll prove the female to my soul,	(6)
	My soul the father; and these two beget	(7)
	A generation of still-breeding thoughts;	(8)
	And these same thoughts people this little world,	(9)
	In humors like the people of this world,	(10)
	For no thought is contented.	(v, v.) (11)

Also from *Richard II*, Bolingbroke condemns Exton, Richard's killer, after having wished the murder done.

Bolingbroke:	They love not poison that do poison need,	(1)
	Nor do I thee. Though I did wish him dead,	(2)

I hate the murderer, love him murdered. (3)
The guilt of conscience take thou for thy labor, (4)
But neither my good word nor princely favor. (5)
With Cain go wander through the shade of night, (6)
And never show thy head by day nor light. (v, vi.) (7)

Note: Line 6 follows the *Folio*. The Pelican edition prefers "through shades of night."

In *As You Like It*, the shepherdess, Phebe, is in love with Rosalind, who is disguised as a man and has rejected her.

Phebe: Think not I love him, though I ask for him; (1)
          'Tis but a peevish boy; yet he talks well. (2)
          But what care I for words? Yet words do well (3)
          When he that speaks them pleases those that hear. (4)
          It is a pretty youth; not very pretty: (5)
          But, sure he's proud, and yet his pride becomes him. (6)
          He'll make a proper man. The best thing in him (7)
          Is his complexion; and faster than his tongue (8)
          Did make offense, his eye did heal it up. (9)
          He is not very tall; yet for his years he's tall. (10)
          His leg is but so so; and yet 'tis well. (11)
          There was a pretty redness in his lip, (12)
          A little riper and more lusty red (13)
          Than that mixed in his cheek; 'twas just the difference (14)
          Betwixt the constant red and mingled damask. (15)
          There be some women, Silvius, had they marked him (16)
          In parcels as I did, would have gone near (17)
          To fall in love with him; but, for my part, (18)
          I love him not nor hate him not; and yet (19)
          I have more cause to hate him than to love him; (20)
          For what had he to do to chide at me? (21)
          He said mine eyes were black and my hair black; (22)
          And, now I am rememb'red, scorned at me. (23)
          I marvel why I answered not again. (24)
          But that's all one: omittance is no quittance. (25)
          I'll write to him a very taunting letter, (26)
          And thou shalt bear it. Wilt thou, Silvius? (27)
Silvius: Phebe, with all my heart. (28)
Phebe: I'll write it straight; (29)
          The matter's in my head and in my heart; (30)

I will be bitter with him and passing short. (31)
Go with me, Silvius. (III, v.) (32)

In this speech, you will find an antithesis not found in the previous two examples.

When lines have no antithetical thoughts, check to see if any ideas are antithetical to something spoken by another person. Note this example from *The Merchant of Venice:*

Bassanio:	This is no answer, thou unfeeling man,	(1)
	To excuse the current of thy cruelty.	(2)
Shylock:	I am not bound to please thee with my answer.	(3)
Bassanio:	Do all men kill the things they do not love?	(4)
Shylock:	Hates any man the thing he would not kill?	(5)
Bassanio:	Every offense is not a hate at first.	(6)
Shylock:	What, wouldst thou have a serpent sting thee twice? (IV, i.)	(7)

In lines 2–7, the idea in each line is antithetical to the next line. You will find many similar exchanges in Shakespeare. Watch for them and play them accordingly. (There is nothing in the answer key about this example.)

You will find many lines and short speeches with no antithetical words, phrases, or thoughts—just straightforward dialogue. In these cases, use the scansion and kick the box.

As a final example, let's look at one sonnet. The sonnets are rich in antithetical words, phrases, and thoughts. They are also rich in imagery, which we will consider in chapter 10.

Sonnet 15

When I consider everything that grows	(1)
Holds in perfection but a little moment,	(2)
That this huge stage presenteth nought but shows	(3)
Whereon the stars in secret influence comment;	(4)
When I perceive that men as plants increase,	(5)
Cheered and checked even by the selfsame sky,	(6)
Vaunt in their youthful sap, at height decrease,	(7)
And wear their brave state out of memory:	(8)
Then the conceit of this inconstant stay	(9)
Sets you most rich in youth before my sight,	(10)
Where wasteful Time debateth with Decay	(11)
To change your day of youth to sullied night;	(12)

And, all in war with Time for love of you,   (13)
As he takes from you, I engraft you new.   (14)

You will discover wonderful antithetical words, phrases, and thoughts in this remarkable sonnet, some of which are included in the answer key.

Hath that awakened you?
Ay, but not frighted me.
THE TAMING OF THE SHREW, V, ii

So pause awhile . . .

Before moving on, take your monologue and sonnet and work out the antithetical words, phrases, and thoughts. It's more fun if you have a few people work with you and have someone check your readings after you've added the antithesis.

USEFUL IDEAS TO REMEMBER:

CHAPTER 9

Text Analysis

By the pricking of my thumbs,
Something wicked this way comes.

MACBETH, IV, i

THE SKILLS WE'VE been working on are part of "analyzing a text." Each of the following skills is a form of analysis:

- Scanning the lines
- Locating where the rhythm breaks
- Using elision and the feminine ending
- Identifying short or shared lines
- Noting caesuras
- Marking the breathing spots
- Supporting final words and phrases (kicking the box)
- Discovering and separating phrases
- Not running thoughts together
- Playing the antithetical words, phrases, and thoughts
- Considering the speech structure
- Understanding the various meanings of each word
- Identifying the imagery

As each of these skills is critical to acting Shakespeare successfully, analysis is not an academic exercise. Only when analysis of the text is completed and the words are spoken aloud should an actor proceed to "character analysis."

ANOTHER DIVERSION

How is analysis tied to playing your action? With Shakespeare, once you know what the language is doing (rhythm changes, antithetical thoughts, etc.) and what it is saying (meaning of all the words, etc.), achieving your objective by playing your action is the same as with realistic text.

There is this difference—in realism, the action you want to play may be buried in the subtext. In Shakespeare, the action is stated in the words themselves. We have returned to a point made earlier: You can't make character choices—including which action to play—until what the language is doing and saying is absolutely clear.

For examples, refer again to "Working with Subtext" on pages 53 to 56.

Complete analysis of a script or sonnet includes even more than the application of those skills that are designed to help us speak the text clearly. It also includes in-depth study of word meanings. Various words had different meanings in the year 1600 than they do now. The actor needs to know as closely as possible what the word meant to Shakespeare, for this will help determine what he intended the line to mean. Immediate sources for these meanings are *The Shakespeare Lexicon* (see bibliography) and the *Oxford English Dictionary*.

Knowing the various ways in which a word might be used leaves the actor freedom of choice. The character will choose the use of the word that helps play the action.

On the other hand, when an actor doesn't bother to dig out the possible meanings of a word and makes an early choice on what the word may mean, the character can become locked into that reading. The action, however, may lead in another direction.

Following is an example of "in-depth" study to determine what is being said in blank verse lines. From the point of view of simply interpreting words and phrases, we will do a basic analysis of *Sonnet 15*. For this analysis, footnotes from various editions, comments from scholars, and personal observations will be used. What each word means or could imply will be worked out.

Begin the text analysis of either scene dialogue or a sonnet by discovering what each word means. Most editions include footnotes that explain unfamiliar words or phrases, but the notes from various editions might differ. Consult at least three.

For analysis of scene dialogue, you will discover that there are hundreds of studies of each of Shakespeare's plays. Some of these are useful to the actor, and a few examples are listed in part 4. You should also be aware of a collection called the "New Variorum Edition," in which the words, lines, and ideas are fully annotated. Each page contains only a few lines of text and a few dozen lines of footnotes. Sometimes the opinions of eight or ten different scholars or directors are quoted.

For analysis of the sonnets, complete annotation is available in numerous critical studies. Two texts will be used here, and both are available to purchase for your personal library. Scholarly texts about the sonnets may seem complex at first. With practice, however, they become quite accessible. For the most part, they trace the usage of a word or phrase, and this can be helpful to the actor. Read through the following examples.

> *I should think this a gull, but that*
> *the white-bearded fellow speaks it.*
> MUCH ADO ABOUT NOTHING, II, iii

DETAILED EXAMPLE

Sonnet 15

When I consider everything that grows	(1)
Holds in perfection but a little moment,	(2)
That this huge stage presenteth nought but shows	(3)
Whereon the stars in secret influence comment;	(4)
When I perceive that men as plants increase,	(5)
Cheered and checked even by the selfsame sky,	(6)
Vaunt in their youthful sap, at height decrease,	(7)
And wear their brave state out of memory:	(8)
Then the conceit of this inconstant stay	(9)
Sets you most rich in youth before my sight,	(10)
Where wasteful Time debateth with Decay	(11)
To change your day of youth to sullied night;	(12)
And, all in war with Time for love of you,	(13)
As he takes from you, I engraft you new.	(14)

First, review the footnotes to the sonnet provided in your text. Then, read the footnotes listed here, as provided in the edition we have used throughout this book, *The Pelican Shakespeare*, edited by Alfred Harbage, and as provided in the HarperCollins edition, *The Complete Works of*

Answers from page 68: line 3, "purses,"—"garments" and "proud,"—"poor"; lines 3/4, "garments poor"—"body rich"; line 4, "mind,"—"body"; line 5, "sun,"—"clouds"; and note that the thoughts in lines 5 and 6 are a simile, not an antithesis.

Shakespeare, edited by David Bevington. The edition also includes all research used for *The Bantam Shakespeare*.

THE PELICAN SHAKESPEARE

Line 3, *stage*—the world
Line 4, *in secret influence comment*—provide a silent commentary by influencing the action
Line 6, *Cheered and checked*—applauded and hissed or nourished and starved
Line 7, *vaunt*—boast
Line 8, *brave*—splendid; *out of memory*—until forgotten
Line 9, *conceit*—idea; *stay*—duration
Line 11, *wasteful*—destructive; *debateth*—joins forces, fights
Line 14, *engraft*—graft, infuse new life into, with poetry. (Harbage, 1455)

HARPERCOLLINS/BANTAM SHAKESPEARE

Line 2, *holds in perfection*—maintains its prime
Line 5, *as*—like
Line 7, *sap*—vigor; *at height decrease*—i.e. no sooner reach full maturity but they (humans) start to decline
Line 9, *conceit*—notion; *inconstant stay*—mutable brief time (on earth)
Line 11, *wasteful . . . Decay*—i.e. Time and Decay contend to see who can ruin you fastest, or join forces to do so, debating between them the best procedure
Line 13, *all in war*—I, fighting with might and main. (Bevington, 1619)

For critical analysis of *Sonnet 15*, the following selections are taken from four pages of notes in *Shakespeare's Sonnets*, edited with commentary by Stephen Booth, and a few examples selected from two pages of notes in *William Shakespeare: The Sonnets and A Lover's Complaint*, edited by John Kerrigan

KERRIGAN: Line 3: *this huge stage presenteth naught but shows.* A renaissance commonplace; compare *As You Like It* II, 7.138-40. 'This wide and universal theatre/Presents more woeful pageants than the scene/Wherein we play in'; and Jaques' reply, 'All the world's a stage . . .'

BOOTH: Line 4: This line is metrically unusual; it asks to be pronounced as a twelve-syllable, six-stress line, and sounds good when pronounced that way. [My note: as an actor reading this sonnet, you must choose between a twelve-syllable line or a feminine ending on "comment." You would probably ignore the twelve-syllable suggestion, elide "influence" to "influ'nce" and select the feminine ending.]

BOOTH: Lines 1-4: The quatrain moves in an appropriately orbital path. It begins with *I consider* and concludes with *the stars . . . comment*; it travels far from its starting place and ends up far from its starting place, but, in a way, the quatrain returns to its starting point, because line 4 can activate the atrophied literal meaning of "to consider": "to look at the stars" (from Latin *cum* and *sidus, sider-*). Lines 3 and 4 are a complicated inversion of *I consider.*

KERRIGAN: Line 4: . . . Renaissance astrologers believed that the *stars* affected men by pouring down an ethereal fluid; this they called *influence.*

BOOTH: Line 6: *Cheered* encouraged ("to cheer" did not yet have its modern and special theatrical meaning, "to shout applause").

BOOTH: Line 7: . . . *at height decrease* having reached their prime, begin to decline *(height* describes the peak of an actor's career—or that of one of the heroes he plays; the full growth of a plant, and the highest point reached by a celestial body in its passage across the sky).

BOOTH: Line 8: And wear their splendid finery *(brave state)* beyond the time when anyone remembers them or the outdated fashions they wear.

BOOTH: Line 10: *Sets you,* places you, that is, evokes your image. *rich in youth* (1) opulent, magnificent during the time of your youthfulness (*in* indicating duration); (2) possessed of abundance of youthfulness (*in* indicating that to which the attribute is limited); (3) richly clothed in youthfulness (*in* expressing relation to that which covers). (Booth, 155–157)

KERRIGAN: Line 12: *sullied night.* The contrast with *day of youth* suggests 'old age, with all its disfigurements' rather than 'death'.

KERRIGAN: Line 13: *all in war* battling with all my might. The poet replaces *Decay* as *Time's* antagonist. (Kerrigan, 192–193)

Where did you study all this goodly speech?
THE TAMING OF THE SHREW, II, i

This research is part of your personal text analysis as itemized on page 73. Now, as you begin rehearsal, nothing is unclear and the choices are at your fingertips. We haven't yet studied imagery, but locating images is also part of your analysis and is the subject of the next chapter.

It may be comforting to know that, for the most part, analyzing sonnets is more difficult than analyzing dramatic text. The ideas and images are more compressed.

This type of analysis for each sonnet and play is available in much more detail in most libraries. Some of the research texts listed in part 4 can easily be added to your personal library.

Discovering the meaning of Shakespeare's language is a world unto itself. Once you enter into it and become excited about the riches hidden there, escape seems impossible. The wealth that you discover is transferred to your character, who, in rehearsal or performance, is supplied with rich, verbal treasures. To apply this type of analysis to your material takes only discipline and time.

So pause awhile …

- Using the edition from which you took your monologue and sonnet, compile the footnotes or endnotes related to your material.
- Obtain at least two other editions of both the monologue and the sonnet, and compile those footnotes.
- Study the analysis of your sonnet from at least two different authors; you may have to choose between numerous interpretations.
- Read the entire play and various analyses of the play from which you selected your monologue.

But thou art deeper read, and better skilled.
TITUS ANDRONICUS, IV, i

USEFUL IDEAS TO REMEMBER:

Answer from page 68: line 2, "prison"—"world"; lines 3/4, "populous"—"myself"; line 5, "cannot do it" to both "hammer it out" (also in line 5) and "compare" in line 6; line 1; line 6, "brain"—"soul"; lines 6/7, "female"—"father"; lines 9/10, "thoughts"—"humors." Antithetical ideas: he will no longer be alone if he can hammer out thoughts into people (the cell will become populous).

CHAPTER 10

Love the Imagery

I ONCE ASKED a fine professional actress what she thought was meant by imagery. She said, "In a text? Well, certain words allow me to draw pictures for the audience—put pictures in their minds. I think that is imagery."

Here is Webster's first definition of imagery: *The formation of mental images.*

The images in Shakespeare's language are expressions of the character's state of mind at that moment. Thousands of papers and books have been written about this subject, and you might want to study some of them at your leisure. For our purposes, remember this: Shakespeare's characters speak what they are thinking, and they communicate much of the time through imagery. That imagery is often a very strong clue to who the character is.

Shakespeare's characters use imagery far more than do the characters in modern plays. They *need* to express themselves through images. In Elizabethan times, the other characters, and the audience, grasped the images. All were on the same page. Nowadays, if you speak in images, much of the audience is likely to be left "in the dark."

Here are a few examples of imagery. In *Romeo and Juliet,* Juliet, a thirteen-year-old girl, uses nine specific images in only seven lines, as she impatiently awaits word of Romeo:

Juliet:	Gallop apace, you fiery-footed steeds,	(1)
	Towards Phoebus' lodging! Such a wagoner	(2)
	As Phaeton would whip you to the west,	(3)
	And bring in cloudy night immediately.	(4)
	Spread thy close curtain, love-performing night,	(5)
	That runaways' eyes may wink, and Romeo	(6)
	Leap to these arms untalked of and unseen.	(III, ii.) (7)

Note the images:
Line 1: "fiery-footed steeds"
Line 2: "Phoebus' lodging" (Phoebus is Apollo as the sun god)
Line 3: "wagoner as Phaeton" (Phaeton is Phoebus' son)
Line 3: "whip you to the west"
Line 4: "cloudy night"
Line 5: "spread thy close curtain"
Line 5: "love-performing night"
Line 6: "runaways' eyes may wink"
Line 7: "Romeo leap to these arms"

In all likelihood, most of the Elizabethan audience understood these images. Surely the actors in the company were familiar with them. Nowadays, comparing something to Phoebus or Phaeton would hardly clarify the idea.

In this example from Act III of *Henry V*, Chorus describes the scene of the King's departure for France.

Chorus:	Thus with imagined wing our swift scene flies,	(1)
	In motion of no less celerity	(2)
	Than that of thought. Suppose that you have seen	(3)
	The well-appointed king at Hampton pier	(4)
	Embark his royalty; and his brave fleet	(5)
	With silken streamers the young Phoebus fanning.	(6)
	Play with your fancies, and in them behold	(7)
	Upon the hempen tackle shipboys climbing;	(8)
	Hear the shrill whistle which doth order give	(9)
	To sounds confused; behold the treaden sails,	(10)
	Borne with th' invisible and creeping wind,	(11)

Answer from page 68: line 1, first phrase to the second phrase; lines 2/3, "wish him dead"—"hate the murderer"; line 3, "hate"—"love" and "murderer"—"murdered"; lines 4/5, "guilt of conscience"—"good word nor princely favor"; lines 6/7, "wander"—"show" and "the shade of night"—"day nor light."

80

> Draw the huge bottoms through the furrowed sea, (12)
> Breasting the lofty surge. (III, i.) (13)

. . . and continuing for a total of thirty-five image-rich lines. Here are the first:

1. The "scene" flying as if on wings
4. "the well-appointed king"
4. "at Hampton pier/Embark"
5. "brave fleet/With silken streamers"
6. "young Phoebus fanning"
8. "hempen tackle" followed by "shipboys climbing"
9. "the shrill whistle"
10. "treaden sails"
11. "invisible and creeping wind"
12. "huge bottoms" followed by "furrowed sea"
13. "breasting the lofty surge"

As a final example, look back at *Sonnet 15* on page 70, and let's concentrate on some of the images.

3. "huge stage" . . . "shows"
4. "stars . . . comment"
7. "vaunt in their youthful sap" (youth boasting); "height decrease" (aged bending)
8. "wear their brave state" (perhaps aged people wearing what is out of fashion; other possibilities as well)
10. "set you most rich in youth" (seeing the one you love in the richness of youth)
11. "Time . . . Decay" (an image which is probably different to each person)
12. "sullied night"
14. "engraft you new"

> *For by the image of my cause I see*
> *The portraiture of his.*
> HAMLET, V, ii

A well-spoken image should create an analogy, an identifiable likeness, in the listener's mind. Nearly every speech in Shakespeare contains images. Use them to help you play your action and achieve your objective.

An image-rich passage is active, not passive. In performance, it engages (or seduces) the listener to participate in the character's action. It is not sentimental, and if you read it too lyrically the listener will lose interest. The imagery must be active and move the action forward.

IMAGERY EXERCISE

With this exercise, the actor experiences what the audience will experience—which is the language, complete with images, coming at the ear. It is not enough for the actor to visualize an image and then use that visualization to help create an emotion to accompany the line reading, a technique which is commonly taught in realistic acting classes. *It is more important that the actor not indulge in applying an emotion, but learn to handle the image vocally so that the audience can experience it as well.*

To practice how to handle the image vocally, apply this exercise to any of Shakespeare's speeches. If a line does not yield an image for you, simply go on to the next line. Not all lines contain clear images.

Look at Chorus's speech from *Henry V* as shown on page 80. Read it aloud once for sense and for the listeners to hear how you read it. Then lie back on the floor, close your eyes, and have someone else read the speech to you—very slowly—without any emphasis or selection of important words. When you hear a word which invokes an image, raise you hand to signal the reader to pause. Concentrate on the image. When you have it in detail, lower your hand to signal the reader to continue—very slowly. Pause at the next image, etc. When you've heard all of the lines, stand and read the speech yourself aloud.

You and the listeners will notice many things. You will try to communicate to the listener the details of the images you have seen. Your articulation and control of the language will improve. You will slow down. You will develop a personal commitment to the images in the speech and a personal ownership of the lines. You will want to make them clear.

This wonderful exercise works every time. You can also use it for realistic text.

You may notice that speeches rich in imagery often have few antithetical words, phrases, or thoughts. Looking at Chorus's same speech, the anti-

Answer from page 69: Here are only a few of the antithetical words, phrases, or thoughts. You should have no trouble picking out the others. Line 1, first phrase against the second phrase; line 2, "peevish boy"—"talks well"; line 3, first phrase against the second phrase; line 4, "speaks"—"hear"; line 5, "is pretty"—"not pretty"; line 6, "proud"—"pride becomes"; lines 8/9 "offense"—"heal" and "tongue"—"eye." There are at least six more in the next twenty-two lines. But note—the second part of the speech, beginning with line 20, is antithetical to the entire first part of the speech. The character appears to reverse direction in the middle of her thoughts. We hadn't seen that reversal in any of the other examples.

thetical words are limited to "motion" and "thought" in lines 2 and 3, "order" and "confused" in lines 9 and 10, and "furrowed" and "lofty" in lines 12 and 13. In Juliet's image-rich speech above, the idea of getting rid of light and bringing on night is antithetical, but there isn't much else.

As an actor, you love words that allow you to draw images. You want to paint pictures in the listeners' minds. Painting pictures helps you to establish who you are, where you are, and what you want. To help you paint those pictures, you won't find better images in dramatic language than Shakespeare's. Love and cherish them!

> *O, woe is me*
> *To have seen what I have seen, see what I see!*
>
> HAMLET, III, i

There are other skills you may want to learn for playing Shakespeare, but we won't study them here. The skills learned in this book prepare you for more advanced work. There are dozens of other exercises which, if practiced, will develop your skills, especially vocal.

Study Cicely Berry's book, *The Actor and the Text*, John Barton's *Playing Shakespeare* (with the accompanying videos), and Kristin Linklater's *Freeing Shakespeare's Voice* or Patsy Rodenburg's *The Need for Words, The Right to Speak* and *The Actor Speaks*. They will help you to improve your Shakespeare.

Do your language study before rehearsals begin, then the rehearsal process can be about character and relationships, as it should be.

A parting thought: no, not "parting is such sweet sorrow," but rather—

> Speak the speech, I pray you, as I pronounced it to you, trippingly on the tongue. But if you mouth it, as many of our players do, I had as lief the town crier spoke my lines. *Hamlet*, III, ii.

> There will be no such mouthing, I pray you . . . *(WV)*

Answers from page 70: Line 3/4, "stage"—"stars" and "shows"—"comment"; line 6, "cheered"—"checked"; line 7, "vaunt"—"decrease" and "youthful"—"height"; line 12, "day" or "day of youth"—"sullied night"; line 13, "war"—"love"; line 14, "takes"—"engraft." Note that the thought of lines 9–14 is antithetical to the thought of lines 1–8. The reader must set up the idea that "time wins every time," so that this thought can be contradicted with "however, my love is such that when time pursues you, my poem makes you immortal in youth."

Thou speak'st
In better phrase and matter than thou didst.

KING LEAR, IV, vi

O, well done! I commend your pains,
And every one shall share i' th' gains.

MACBETH, IV, i

USEFUL IDEAS TO REMEMBER:

PART TWO

For Secondary Schools: Reading Shakespeare Aloud

I have studied eight or nine wise words to speak to you,

MUCH ADO ABOUT NOTHING, III, ii

CHAPTER 11

Reading Shakespeare Aloud

IN THIS CHAPTER, selected material from part 1 is condensed for secondary English and drama teachers, and students who may not have time to study the complete book. High school students could begin their Shakespeare studies with this chapter. Shakespeare reading groups and persons who simply enjoy reading the plays and poems could also begin here. When more detailed instruction is needed, refer to part 1.

Worksheets are included. These may be enlarged and reproduced so that each reader or student has a copy. Combined with the worksheets, a teacher might use this chapter as an outline for a unit of instruction on Shakespeare. Selected scenes and monologues suitable for student practice are listed.

While studying specific skills, examples of film and video performances as noted in part 4 may be helpful. For the student who wants additional study, many useful works are included in the bibliography.

What is the end of study, let me know?
LOVE'S LABOR'S LOST, I, i

PREPARATION

Many people do not realize that Shakespeare is meant to be read or spoken aloud. Not only is the work better aloud, it is ten times better! By learning only a few reading (and acting) skills, anyone can read and enjoy the plays, sonnets, and poems.

Most Shakespearean studies concentrate on one of these:
- "Meaning" of the thoughts, metaphors, or imagery
- The historical significance of specific events as they relate to the plays
- Analysis of characters—why do they do this or that?

These types of studies are important and will help you as an actor or reader. They are especially helpful when acting or reading a "realistic" play, which means a play with language written like modern speech. On the other hand, with a Shakespearean play, that research and background won't help you in the same way.

Background knowledge is useful only *after* you've taken a preliminary step not usually necessary with a realistic play. With Shakespeare, or any play written in "heightened" language—which is language composed with a specific rhythmic pattern—you must first learn *what* the language is doing and read it according to its rhythm and meter. If you don't first learn the skills required to speak the language, information from other studies won't do you one bit of good, because the listener will have no idea what you are saying.

You may already believe that Shakespeare is too difficult to understand. Perhaps you have heard it read aloud, or read it aloud yourself, and concluded that it makes no sense. If that is the case, you are simply reading without applying the speaking skills required to clarify the language, or you are hearing someone else read who is not using the skills. Of course, once you've learned the skills, any background information can and should be used to make your reading or acting as complete and truthful as possible. But first you must know and use the speaking skills.

Here is a helpful analogy: You want to play a song on the piano. You bang away at the keys, but don't know which ones to hit. How many listeners will recognize the song? With Shakespeare, the words are the notes. Hit the right notes, and the listener will know what you mean.

FOUR SIMPLE SKILLS

The key to reading Shakespeare aloud is knowing which words to emphasize. Selecting these words is really quite simple, and the following easy-to-learn skills will get you started. If this information is completely new to you, don't feel alone. Most people, including many actors, haven't a clue how to do this. But if you use these four skills and read the verse aloud, it will make sense:

- Support the final word in each line
- Emphasize the stressed words or syllables
- Separate the thoughts (phrasing)
- Breathe only at punctuation points

Follow these simple guidelines and discover that Shakespeare is, indeed, better—a lot better—than it might have first seemed. It is, in fact, remarkably beautiful.

SIMPLE BREATHING WARMUP

When working on Shakespeare (or any dramatic text), it's helpful to be relaxed and breathing properly. You want your breathing to be deep and fill the lungs. To experience that feeling, lie on your back on the floor, arms at your sides, knees raised, and breathe deeply in through your nose, out through your mouth. As your lungs fill, you will feel your lower back press into the floor. Establish a slow breath in/breath out rhythm. Notice how easy it is to concentrate. Allow your focus to become concentrated. Now memorize what your muscles are doing to fill your lungs with air. When you sit or stand up, try to keep that muscle group working and your breathing deep.

Now you're ready to read this language. (And here is an added benefit: If you read some of the lines while lying on your back and breathing correctly, you will notice how nicely your voice lowers in pitch and fills out in resonance.)

FIRST SKILL: SUPPORT THE FINAL WORD IN EACH LINE

The end of the blank verse line is usually more important than the beginning or middle. (Blank verse is explained in the next section.) When reading Shakespeare aloud, support the end of the line—including both the final phrase and final word—and notice the sudden clarity. This speaking style is dramatically opposed to the modern tendency to allow lines to fade away, like songs without endings.

For example, here is Portia speaking to Shylock in the courtroom scene of *The Merchant of Venice*.

Portia: The quality of mercy is not strained,   (*MV*, IV, i)

Read the line aloud, and let the second phrase ("is not strained") fall away so that you can barely hear it. When read that way, the line seems to be about something called "mercy" and something else we aren't quite sure about.

Now read the line aloud a second time, and support the second phrase ("is not strained") with equal or more power than you give the first phrase ("The quality of mercy"), and be certain to emphasize the final word "strained." What is the line about? Now it's about a quality called "mercy," which is not obtained by "straining" at it. Now the line makes sense.

Romeo has this response to Friar Laurence's counseling:

Romeo: Thou canst not speak of that thou dost not feel.   (*Rom*, III, iii)

Read the line aloud and let the final word "feel" drop away so you can barely hear it. What is the line about? Romeo is telling the Friar he can't speak. Now read the line aloud again and support the word "feel." What is the line about? Romeo may be telling the Friar, who is presumed celibate, that he has never known the love of a woman, so how can he counsel? Now the line is rich with possibilities.

Try this very effective exercise. Select a few lines of verse—there are examples in Skill Worksheet #1, beginning on page 100—then place a cardboard box on the floor in front of you. Be sure that each line you select consists of ten syllables. We'll work on eleven- and twelve-syllable lines in the next section.

As you read the lines, kick the box on the final syllable of each ten-syllable line. Kicking the box puts energy into your reading, allows your entire body to become involved, and forces you to support the end of the line. Kick on exactly the final syllable. Using Romeo's line, don't kick on "not," and don't kick after "feel." Kick on the *f* of "feel." On Portia's line, kick on the *s* of "strained." Practice this skill with other lines, and you'll soon discover that supporting the final word through use of the diaphragm becomes second nature. You will notice that people listen to you.

Refer to Skill Worksheet #1 on page 100 for other practice lines and speeches. Check the index for more detailed study of this skill.

SECOND SKILL: EMPHASIZE THE STRESSED WORDS OR SYLLABLES

To make your reading even more understandable, add this second skill. Blank verse—which is a form of writing the English language in ten-syllable lines, not necessarily rhyming—has a specific rhythm, which identifies the important words.

Each pair of syllables creates one "foot." So the blank verse line has five "feet." Each foot has a soft stress and a hard stress. Think of your own foot: The heel is soft, and the ball is hard. When you walk, the rhythm is soft/hard, soft/hard, soft/hard, and so on. Try it and speak the rhythm aloud. In blank verse, this rhythm becomes dee dum, dee dum, dee dum, dee dum, dee dum—five feet, five soft stresses, five hard stresses, one blank verse line. This type of line is called iambic pentameter.*

Most scholars and stage directors agree that blank verse is the closest written expression of English speech. Without realizing it, you speak blank verse all the time. For example, "What would you like to do this afternoon?" and "Let's go to town and buy an ice cream cone" are two lines of blank verse! For your own enjoyment, converse for awhile in blank verse, and write some original lines.

Breaking a blank verse line into feet and marking the stresses is called scanning the line, or scansion. Here is Romeo gazing at Juliet's balcony:

But soft! What light through yonder window breaks?   (*Rom*, II, ii)

Break the line into five feet, two syllables per foot:

But soft! / What light / through yon / der win / dow breaks?

Now mark the stresses, ⌣ for soft, / for hard:

⌣   /   ⌣   /   ⌣   /   ⌣ /   ⌣   /
But soft! / What light / through yon / der win / dow breaks?

When you read the line aloud, stress the hard syllables: "soft," "light," "yon," "win," "breaks." With your hand, beat out these stressed words or syllables on the table or chair, while you read the line aloud three or four times. Then forget scansion and read the line naturally.

Notice that you still give a slight emphasis to the stressed words. Your goal is to achieve naturalness and honesty, while stressing the correct words. By *not* achieving this goal, you unintentionally disguise the meaning of the line. To prove this point, read the line aloud and emphasize the soft syllables: "But," "What," "through," "der," "dow." Notice the problem? That is what happens if you emphasize the wrong word or words.

Shakespeare's language is written in this *regular* "dee dum, dee dum" rhythm, with effects achieved by use of *irregular* lines. For example, a word to be stressed might be placed in the unstressed position, or an eleventh

---

*See *iamb* and *iambic pentameter* in the Glossary of Terms.

syllable—a "dee" without a "dum"—might be added. Here's an example of breaking the rhythm in the opening speech of *Romeo and Juliet*.

Chorus:	Two households, both alike in dignity,	(1)
	In fair Verona, where we lay our scene,	(2)
	From ancient grudge, break to new mutiny,	(3)
	Where civil blood makes civil hands unclean.	(*Rom*, Pro) (4)

Lines 1, 2, and 4 are regular blank verse lines; but notice line 3. First, separate the line into feet:

From an / cient grudge / break to / new mut / in y,

In the third foot, the verb "break" (in the non-stressed position) is more important than the preposition "to" (in the stressed position). The stress in that foot is inverted, and you must read it accordingly. This type of foot is called a trochaic foot, or trochee, rather than an iambic foot.

Read the line aloud twice, first emphasizing "to," then emphasizing "break." How do you know when a word breaks the rhythm? Scan the line, and with a little practice, your common sense will tell you.

For example, in the fourth foot of the same line, you could argue that "new" also breaks the rhythm and is as important as "mut." That's a good argument, because it points out that an earlier mutiny is starting over again. Read it aloud twice, once each way, then choose the way which seems right to you.

You might also argue that, in line 1, "Two" is as important as "house." That's a reader choice, but could be a good one, because it clarifies the number of families involved in the fray. Lines often have three or more stresses back-to-back (there are even lines with ten stressed syllables), as this line has "Two," "house," and "holds," all of which you could choose to stress.

In each case, scan the line to decide if and where the rhythm breaks, then speak accordingly. If you decided to stress "Two," "holds," and "new," the lines would scan like this:

Two house / holds, both / a like / in dig / ni ty

In fair / Ver o / na, where / we lay / our scene,

From an / cient grudge, / break to / new mut / i ny,

Where civ / il blood / makes civ / il hands / un clean.

The next example, the most famous line in Shakespeare, illustrates an added syllable—a "dee" without a "dum"—as Hamlet contemplates action.

To be, or not to be—that is the question:　　　(*Ham*, III, i)

The line scans like this:

$$\overset{\smile}{\text{To be,}} / \overset{/}{} \overset{\smile}{\text{or not}} / \overset{/}{} \overset{\smile}{\text{to be}}— / \overset{\smile}{\text{that is}} / \overset{/}{} \overset{\smile}{\text{the ques}} / \overset{(\smile)}{\text{tion:}}$$

To be, / or not / to be— / that is / the ques / tion:

This line has eleven syllables and calls for a soft or unstressed ending. This "feminine" ending, used throughout Shakespeare, allows a line to end without a stressed syllable. You kick the box on "ques-"—not on "-tion." Let "-tion" just be there, giving the line a soft ending.

When scanning a blank verse line, if you don't count ten syllables and five feet, you may be looking at a feminine ending. But another possibility is to change the eleven-syllable line to ten by eliding two syllables or words into one. For example, "I will" becomes "I'll" and is spoken as one syllable.

For another example, in the following eleven-syllable line, Shakespeare has already elided a two-syllable word into one syllable, but the reader must elide another word, as "man" is stressed and would not make a feminine ending.

Hamlet:　Horatio, thou art e'en as just a man.　　　(*Ham*, III, ii)

Note "even" is already elided to "e'en" and pronounced as one syllable. The reader must elide "Horatio" to "Horat'o," pronounced as three syllables. Now the line can be spoken in ten syllables with correct rhythm.

Hor a / t'o, thou / art e'en / as just / a man.

In the previous line, "question" is not spoken with emphasis on the second syllable; it can be a feminine-ending line. But "man" is a stressed word, so you must find an elision somewhere in the line to compress it to ten syllables. Often feminine-ending words end in "-ing," "-en," and "-tion."

See Skill Worksheet #2 on page 102 for more examples of elision and for practice lines and speeches. If you want more study of this skill, check the index.

THIRD SKILL: SEPARATE THE THOUGHTS

You now have two skills for reading Shakespeare: (1) supporting the end of the line and (2) scanning to emphasize the stressed words and rhythm changes. There's a third skill, phrasing, which is no more difficult than the first two. All blank verse lines can be divided into phrases. When you read aloud, separate the phrases slightly. Each phrase is a thought; if you run the thoughts together the listener gets lost.

Many phrases are separated by punctuation marks. When there is no punctuation, separate each phrase with a slight pause. This pause is called a caesura (si-zhoor´-ə), meaning a "sense pause." This is not a "breath" pause; it's much shorter. It is just a slight pause that allows the ear to hear an emphasis placed on the phrase or word you just said or are about to say.

If you use the caesura (marked //) to practice separating phrases, then forget the pauses and speak naturally, you will notice that, even when speaking rapidly, the phrases have been embedded in your mind as individual thoughts, and you will automatically handle each separately. In this next example, Brutus's answer to Cassius, after hearing the suggestion that Caesar has grown too strong, is broken into phrases by inserting caesuras. Where a phrase is already identified by punctuation, a caesura is not inserted.

Brutus:	What you have said //	(1)
	I will consider; what you have to say //	(2)
	I will with patience hear; and find a time //	(3)
	Both meet to hear and answer // such high things.	(4)
	Till then, my noble friend, chew upon this:	(5)
	Brutus had rather be a villager //	(6)
	Than to repute himself a son of Rome //	(7)
	Under these hard conditions // as this time	(8)
	Is like to lay upon us.	(*JC*, I, ii) (9)

Work on the speech, separating the thoughts as marked (some readers and actors prefer to circle the phrases rather than to use caesura marks), then forget the marks, and read the speech naturally.

You should discover that you give individuality to each thought, regardless of how quickly you speak. (The final line is called a "short line," meaning that either a pause sufficient to complete the ten-syllable rhythm is intended, or the line is finished by the next speaker. In this case, Cassius will finish the line with "I am glad," to make ten syllables.)

At this point you might create an exercise designed to focus the reader's attention on separation of phrases. *Read aloud from punctuation point to punctuation point* (which are also your breathing points), and force yourself to stop at each point. Give the reader something to do at each point. For example, read lines 1 and 2, up to the word "consider." (Note that the line contains two phrases, as do other lines that follow, but only walk and breathe at punctuation points.) Then walk silently to another spot in the room before reading the next line, which ends on "hear." Then walk silently to another spot in the room, and so forth. Moving between the punctuation points causes you to consider what you *have* said and what you *will* say as separate thoughts. After reading the speech with the thoughts separated, forget the moving, and read the speech naturally.

Separating phrases separates individual thoughts. You must also watch for shorter phrases within longer ones. For example, "Under these hard conditions" is a shorter phrase within the longer one, which includes all of lines 6–9. You may want to expand the exercise to move on these inside phrases as well. Once the phrases are separated, it will be easy to discover different interpretations for the individual thoughts and then to select the reading you like.

Refer to Skill Worksheet #3 on page 106 for additional phrasing exercises. If you want more study of the phrasing skill, refer to the index.

FOURTH SKILL: BREATHE ONLY AT PUNCTUATION POINTS

Added to the three skills you've now learned—kicking the box, scanning the line, and phrasing— remember to breathe at the right places. When reading Shakespeare, random breathing can destroy the sense of the line, because the misplaced pause for a breath fractures the thought.

A reliable guide is this: Breathe at the punctuation points. Don't breathe at the end of a phrase (as in Brutus's lines 1, 2, 3, 6, 7, and 8) unless the phrase ends with a punctuation mark (as in the middle of lines 3, 4, 5, and 9). The speech appears in worksheets #3 and #5 on pages 106 and 115.

Verse lines are often *enjambed*, which means the thought in the line continues to the next line without pause or punctuation. Shakespeare's lines are more often than not enjambed. Brutus's speech above has end-of-line punctuation (and breathing points) only on lines 4 and 5. The other lines require breathing at the punctuation points *within* the lines. In Macbeth's speech below, all lines are enjambed except 1, 2, and 4. Line 10 is enjambed into 11, because it continues "He chid the sisters/When first they put the name of King upon me."

In this example, Macbeth, having killed the king, now contemplates killing his friend, Banquo.

Macbeth:	To be thus is nothing, but to be safely thus—	(1)
	Our fears in Banquo stick deep,	(2)
	And in his royalty of nature reigns that	(3)
	Which would be feared. 'Tis much he dares;	(4)
	And to that dauntless temper of his mind	(5)
	He hath a wisdom that doth guide his valour	(6)
	To act in safety. There is none but he	(7)
	Whose being I do fear; and under him	(8)
	My genius is rebuked, as it is said	(9)
	Mark Antony's was by Caesar. (*Mac*, III, i.)	(10)

This speech contains typical Shakespearean punctuation. The breathing points are the punctuation marks. Circle them, and then read the speech aloud, breathing at each mark. You will find that it is quite easy to speak from one breathing point to the next. The longest stretch is two and one-half lines. (In the previous Brutus speech, the longest stretch is three and one-half lines.)

Don't breathe after "Banquo" in line 2 (the end of a thought), but after "deep," and take the pause needed to finish the rhythm of this short line. Don't breathe after "that" in line 3 (the end of the verse line on paper), but try it once to discover the problem for yourself. Likewise, try breathing after "mind," "valour," "he," "him," and "said." Your common sense and good ear will tell you that the choice is wrong.

You might want to practice an exercise to focus your attention on breathing correctly. This works effectively: At each punctuation point, whether you have spoken one word or four lines, exhale all unused breath, then fill your lungs with a deep breath before speaking the next line. Do this at each punctuation point. Do not hurry, or you may sense dizziness. Concentrate on making yourself take the time to breathe deeply and fill the lungs before continuing. Try not to take little gasping breaths that fill only one-third of your lung capacity. After doing the exercise, read the speech naturally, and notice that you automatically breathe more deeply at the appropriate points. Reserve breath gives you power; running out of breath signals weakness.

In Skill Worksheet #4 on page 110 are a few more good speeches for breathing practice. For more advanced study, check the index.

A CONCLUDING NOTE

When reading Shakespeare, it's natural to want to "act it out." Readers will often "enhance" the language with sounds, gasps, crying, whispering, pauses for effect, sighs, and "ahs." Such enhancements tend to destroy the rhythm. When the rhythm is lost, the thoughts—and the audience—are also lost.

Overpowering blank verse with emotion because "my character would do this" simply doesn't work. Your reading becomes indulgent, because you've lost *what* is being said in favor of *how* it is being said. Generally this direction works: If you want to cry, cry after the line, not during the line. We must hear the words first, then we can experience your sorrow without the irritation caused by a muffled line.

The emotions needed by the character are already written into the verse. All you have to do is speak the lines honestly by using your newly-acquired reading/acting skills. These four skills are all you need to begin enjoying Shakespeare. Have fun!

I have some private schooling for you both.

A MIDSUMMER NIGHT'S DREAM, I, i

MORE ADVANCED STUDY

When reading Shakespeare aloud, the language will make sense if you use the four skills you've just learned. The meaning of most lines will be clear. There is, of course, more to learn. For advanced training, here are a few more skills. Refer to the index for more study of each.

Learn to handle antithesis, which is placing one word or thought against an opposite word or thought—like "To be" (one thought) "or not to be" (an opposite thought). Shakespeare is full of antithesis, and you will read better if you can identify the antithetical thoughts and play them. For more information and some exercises, see Skill Worksheet #5 on page 115.

Practice using elision. Lines often have eleven or twelve syllables. Sometimes they are feminine-ending lines, but sometimes words or pairs of words must be elided, or condensed together, so the rhythm will work. Some examples are included in Skill Worksheet #6 on page 118 and the Glossary of Terms.

Learn about the structure of speeches. The pattern is usually (1) introduction of an idea, (2) development, and (3) conclusion or summary.

Identify the imagery. Unlike modern playwrights, Shakespeare's language is rich in images and metaphors—like Romeo's ". . . Juliet is the sun" or Juliet's "Gallop apace you fiery-footed steeds."

Learn to analyze the text. Study what others before you have discovered about the meaning of specific words, ideas, and references. Write out a speech or sonnet in your own words.

Learn the acting skill of saying what you think when you think it. This skill is unlike the acting approach that allows you to think about the thought, *then* speak the subtext. See part 1, chapter 6 for work on this skill and also on playing your action to achieve your objective.

Many of the basic skills learned for acting realistic texts can be applied to Shakespeare, especially the skills of playing your action to achieve your objective and staying in the moment. Listen to what the other character is saying, and respond honestly to that, don't plan ahead. For more training, see part 4 and the bibliography of books available on acting Shakespeare. If you become interested in this greatest of all writers, consulting some of these works will be both exciting and rewarding. Enjoy the Bard!

USEFUL IDEAS TO REMEMBER:

CHAPTER 12

Worksheets

NOTE:

These worksheets may be enlarged and reproduced without author permission. Answers are included following the exercises for each skill.

SKILL WORKSHEET I

SUPPORT THE FINAL WORD OF EACH LINE ("KICK THE BOX")

A. Here are the two examples used in the chapter:

Portia: The quality of mercy is not strained;   (*MV*, iv, i)

Romeo: Thou canst not speak of that thou dost not feel.   (*Rom*, iii, iii)

B. Here are other speeches with which to practice. The first three examples are from *Julius Caesar*.

1. Portia speaks to Brutus after the conspirators have left. Kick the box on the last syllable of each line. However, one line has a feminine ending, so kick on the tenth syllable of that line.

Portia: You have some sick offense within your mind,
            Which by the right and virtue of my place
            I ought to know of; and upon my knees
            I charm you, by my once-commended beauty,
            By all your vows of love, and that great vow
            Which did incorporate and make us one,   (*JC*, ii, i)

2. Calphurnia speaks to Caesar. Kick on the final syllable of each line. However, one line has a feminine ending, so kick on the tenth syllable of that line. Also, in one line, a one-syllable word must be spoken as two syllables to keep the rhythm.

Calphurnia: Caesar, I never stood on ceremonies,
            Yet now they fright me. There is one within,
            Besides the things that we have heard and seen,
            Recounts most horrid sights seen by the watch.
            A lioness hath whelped in the streets,
            And graves have yawned and yielded up their dead.   (*JC*, ii, ii)

3. Here is Mark Antony alone with Caesar's body. Again, kick on the final syllable of each line. However, once again, one line has a feminine ending, so kick on the tenth syllable of the line. Also, in two different lines, a one-syllable word must be spoken as two syllables to keep the rhythm.

Antony: O, pardon me, thou bleeding piece of earth,
            That I am meek and gentle with these butchers!

Thou art the ruin of the noblest man
That ever lived in the tide of times.   (*JC*, III, i)

4. Here is an example from *Romeo and Juliet*. The Nurse is speaking to
Lady Capulet about Juliet's age.

Nurse: Even or odd, of all days in the year,
           Come Lammas Eve at night shall she be fourteen.
           Susan and she (God rest all Christian souls!)
           Were of an age. Well, Susan is with God;
           She was too good for me. But, as I said,
           On Lammas Eve at night shall she be fourteen;
           That shall she, marry; I remember it well.   (*Rom*, I, iii)

In this speech, kick on the tenth and final syllable of each line. However, two of the lines have feminine endings, so in these lines, kick on the
tenth syllable. Also, in one line, you must practice *elision* (combining two
words into one—e.g., "I will" into "I'll,"—or removing a vowel from a word
to shorten it, as "int'rest" for "interest"). This is done so that you can read
the line with fewer syllables and make the rhythm work. There are more
examples of elision in Skill Worksheet #6.

Practice the kick box exercise with any verse lines of Shakespeare. Be
sure to check for feminine endings and elision to keep the rhythm, then
kick on the tenth syllable.

TIPS AND ANSWERS FOR SKILL WORKSHEET I

B. 1. You were correct if you selected "beauty" for the feminine ending and
kicked on the first syllable of the word.

2. Selecting "ceremonies" as the feminine ending and "whelped" to be
spoken with two syllables ("whelp'ed") would be correct.

3. "Butchers" is the feminine ending. Both "ruin" and "lived" must be
spoken with two syllables: "ru-in" and "liv'ed."

4. In this speech, each "fourteen" is a feminine ending. Elide the *e* from
the final syllable of "remember" and combine with "it" to get "re mem
b'rit," eliding from four to three syllables. Now you can keep the rhythm.
The line would scan:

That shall / she mar / ry; I / re mem / b'rit well.

SKILL WORKSHEET 2

SCANSION: EMPHASIZE STRESSED WORDS OR SYLLABLES

A. Here are the three examples used in the chapter. For practice, mark the scansion of these lines as you worked it out on page 91. Circle words that break the rhythm.

Romeo:	But soft! What light through yonder window breaks? (*Rom*, II, ii)

Chorus:	Two households, both alike in dignity,
	In fair Verona, where we lay our scene,
	From ancient grudge, break to new mutiny,
	Where civil blood makes civil hands unclean. (*Rom*, Pro)

Hamlet:	To be, or not to be—that is the question: (*Ham*, III, i)

B. Here are three practice speeches. Mark the scansion of these lines. All are regular blank verse lines of ten syllables, two syllables per foot.

1. The first is Helena to her companions in *A Midsummer Night's Dream*:

Helena:	O Spite! O hell! I see you all are bent
	To set against me for your merriment.
	If you were civil and knew courtesy,
	You would not do me thus much injury. (III, ii)

2. Here is Juliet to the Friar in *Romeo and Juliet*:

Juliet:	Conceit, more rich in matter than in words,
	Brags of his substance, not of ornament.
	They are but beggars that can count their worth;
	But my true love is grown to such excess
	I cannot sum up sum of half my wealth. (II, vi)

3. In the same play, Mercutio to Romeo:

Mercutio:	O, then I see Queen Mab hath been with you.
	She is the fairies' midwife, and she comes
	In shape no bigger than an agate stone
	On the forefinger of an alderman, (I, iv)

C. The next two examples require more thought. Mark the feet, the stressed words, and any words that break the rhythm.

   1. Puck to the Fairies in *A Midsummer Night's Dream*:

Puck: The King doth keep his revels here tonight.
          Take heed the Queen come not within his sight.
          For Oberon is passing fell and wrath,
          Because that she, as her attendant, hath
          A lovely boy, stolen from an Indian King;   (II, i)

In one line, there are twelve syllables without a feminine ending, so you must elide two. See if you can do it. One word breaks the rhythm.

   2. Here is Antonio's opening speech in *The Merchant of Venice*.

Antonio: In sooth I know not why I am so sad.
          It worries me, you say it worries you;
          But how I caught it, found it, or came by it,
          What stuff 'tis made of, whereof it is born,
          I am to learn;
          And such a want-wit sadness makes of me
          That I have much ado to know myself.   (I, i)

One elision is necessary. One word might be emphasized to break the rhythm. One line is a "short line." See if you can figure out how to read it.

D. Take any of Shakespeare's verse lines and practice marking the feet, then the stressed syllables, the feminine endings, the words that break the rhythm, and any words that must be elided to keep the rhythm.

TIPS AND ANSWERS FOR SKILL WORKSHEET 2

B. 1. All are regular lines. Each two syllables makes one foot for five feet per line.

$$\breve{O} \text{ spite! } / \acute{O} \text{ hell! } / \breve{I} \text{ see } / \text{you all } / \text{are bent}$$

$$\text{To set } / \text{a gainst } / \text{me for } / \text{your mer } / \text{ri ment.}$$

$$\text{If you } / \text{were civ } / \text{il and } / \text{knew cour } / \text{te sy,}$$

$$\text{You would } / \text{not do } / \text{me thus } / \text{much in } / \text{ju ry.}$$

2. All are regular lines, two syllables per foot, five feet. Notice that "Brags" and "true" break the rhythm.

Con ceit, / more rich / in mat / ter than / in words,

Brags of / his sub / stance, not / of orn / a ment.

They are / but beg / gars that / can count / their worth;

But my / true love / is grown / to such / ex cess

I can / not sum / up sum / of half / my wealth.

"Brags" is an action verb, more important than "of." Line 4 can also be read as a regular line, with "true" unstressed. But doesn't it work better if you stress it? You might also choose to stress "But."

3. All are regular lines, five feet. Notice that "O," "Queen," and "fore" break the rhythm.

O, then / I see / Queen Mab / hath been / with you.

She is / the fair / ies' mid / wife, and / she comes

In shape / no big / ger than / an ag / ate stone

On the / fore fin / ger of / an al / der man,

C. 1.

The King / doth keep / his rev / els here / to night.

Take heed / the Queen / come not / with in / his sight.

For O / ber on / is pass / ing fell / and wrath,

Be cause / that she, / as her / at tend / ant, hath

A love / ly boy, / stol'n from / an In / d'an King;

To make a ten-syllable line of the final line, elide "stolen" (which also breaks the rhythm) to one syllable (stol'n) and "Indian" to two syllables ("Ind'an"). Now the rhythm works.

2. In line 3, elide "by it" to "by't." Line 5 is a "short line" that calls for a pause of three feet (dee dum dee dum dee dum) to complete the rhythm before you read line 6. (Short lines may also be completed by the next speaker, but that isn't the case here.) In line 3, "came" may break the rhythm, if you choose that reading.

In sooth / I know / not why / I am / so sad.

It wor / ries me, / you say / it wor / ries you;

But how / I caught / it found / it or / <u>came</u> by't,

What stuff / 'tis made / of, where / of it / is born,

I am / to learn; / (dee dum) / (dee dum) / (dee dum)

And such / a want- / wit sad / ness makes / of me

That I / have much / a do / to know / my self.

SKILL WORKSHEET 3

PHRASING: SEPARATE THE THOUGHTS

A. Once readers learn to phrase, they will not rush the language. Many phrases are identified by the punctuation marks. Others must be discovered. Watch for where the thought changes.

Here is the example that was worked out on page 94, as Brutus answers Cassius. For practice, circle the phrases or mark them by use of the caesura (//).

Brutus:	What you have said	(1)
	I will consider; what you have to say	(2)
	I will with patience hear; and find a time	(3)
	Both meet to hear and answer such high things.	(4)
	Till then, my noble friend, chew upon this:	(5)
	Brutus had rather be a villager	(6)
	Than to repute himself a son of Rome	(7)
	Under these hard conditions as this time	(8)
	Is like to lay upon us.	(*JC*, 1, ii.) (9)

B. Read the following speeches and mark all phrases. You might also do the complete scansion.

1. The first is Richard III's opening monologue. Richard is not yet king, but covets the throne. Blocking his way are his two brothers: the present King Edward IV, who has two sons of his own, and Clarence. Yet, with the House of York returned to the throne through war, Richard is closer to his goal than he has ever been.

Richard:	Now is the winter of our discontent	
	Made glorious summer by this son of York;	
	And all the clouds that lowered upon our house	
	In the deep bosom of the ocean buried.	(*RIII*, 1, i.)

Here is the speech broken into phrases by use of the caesura (//), with shorter phrases or breaks within the phrases marked with one /. Too many phrases would be wrong for performance, of course, but can be very right for reading and rehearsal, as the phrases force the reader to separate the thoughts. (Scansion is shown in the Tips and Answers.)

Now / is the winter // of our / discontent //
Made / glorious summer // by this / son of York;

And / all the clouds // that lowered / upon our house //
In the deep bosom // of the ocean / buried.

Note that the first phrase, "Now is the winter," contains two thoughts, not one: "Now" and "is the winter." When practicing phrasing, consider various possibilities for each thought. For example, "Now" could mean right now at this moment, now as a period of time, now after something else has passed, now as opposed to later, and so on. The phrase "is the winter" could mean winter of the year, the latter part of life, a coldness, a desolate time, the opposite of summer, and so on. Once you have considered the many possibilities for each thought, select one and try it. Then try others until you are satisfied with the reading. What you are doing is determining the possibilities within the language *before* you decide *how* to read the line and *before* you make character decisions. This approach will help you make strong choices.

2. These are Capulet's orders to Tybalt, who has recognized Romeo in disguise at the Capulet party and wants to challenge him.

Capulet: Content thee, gentle cuz, let him alone.
           'A bears him like a portly gentleman,
           And, to say truth, Verona brags of him
           To be a virtuous and well-governed youth.
           I would not for the wealth of all this town
           Here in my house do him disparagement.
           It is my will, the which if you respect,
           Show a fair presence and put off these frowns,
           An ill-beseeming semblance for a feast.   (*Rom*, I, iv.)

3. In this speech, Romeo asks the Apothecary for poison.

Romeo: Come hither, man. I see that thou art poor.
          Hold, there is forty ducats. Let me have
          A dram of poison, such soon-speeding gear
          As will disperse itself through all the veins
          That the life-weary taker may fall dead,
          And that the trunk may be discharged of breath
          As violently as hasty powder fired
          Doth hurry from the fatal cannon's womb.   (*Rom*, v, i)

4. Here is Brutus (the commander) to Cassius (one of his generals) in the battle that follows the murder of Caesar in *Julius Caesar:*

Brutus: Remember March; the ides of March remember.
            Did not great Julius bleed for justice sake?
            What villain touched his body that did stab
            And not for justice? What, shall one of us,
            That struck the foremost man of all this world
            But for supporting robbers—shall we now
            Contaminate our fingers with base bribes,
            And sell the mighty space of our large honors
            For so much trash as may be grasped thus?   (iv, iii)

5. In one of Hamlet's soliloquies, study the four lines without punctuation, and circle the many phrases within them.

Hamlet: To be, or not to be—that is the question:
            Whether 'tis nobler in the mind to suffer
            The slings and arrows of outrageous fortune
            Or to take arms against a sea of troubles
            And by opposing end them.   (*Ham,* III, i)

6. In this final example, mark the phrases as Theseus asks for a play to be performed in *A Midsummer Night's Dream.*

Theseus: Come now, what masques, what dances shall we have,
            To wear away this long age of three hours
            Between our after-supper and bedtime?
            Where is our usual manager of mirth?
            What revels are in hand? Is there no play
            To ease the anguish of a torturing hour?   (v, i)

For additional study of phrasing, refer to the index and the appropriate chapters in the main text.

TIPS AND ANSWERS FOR SKILL WORKSHEET 3

B.1.

Now is / the win / ter of / our dis / con tent

Made glo / ri'us sum / mer by / this son / of York;
(Elide "glorious" to "glori'us," pronounced as two syllables.)

˘ / ˘ / ˘ / ˘ / ˘ /
And all / the clouds / that lower'd / u pon / our house
(Elide "lowered" to "lower'd," spoken as one syllable.)

˘ ˘ / / ˘ / ˘ / ˘ / (˘)
In the / deep bo / som of / the o / cean bur / ied.
(A feminine ending.)

2. Phrase endings not identified by punctuation: after "him," line 3; "virtuous," line 4; "not" and "town," line 5; "house," line 6; "presence," line 7; and "semblance," line 8. For scansion, in line 4, elide "virtuous" to "virt'ous." All lines except 8 are regular. "Show" breaks the rhythm.

3. Phrase endings are "gear," line 3; "itself" and "veins," line 4; "taker," line 5; "trunk" and "breath," line 6; "fired," line 7. "Hold" and "life" break the rhythm. For scansion, line 7 has twelve syllables. Elide "violently" to "vi'lently" and "fired" to "fir'd," or let it have a feminine ending. All others are regular lines.

4. Phrase endings are "bleed," line 2; "body," line 3; "man" and "world," line 5; "fingers," line 7; "space" and "honors," line 8; and "trash," line 9. In line 8, "large" breaks the rhythm. For scansion, the second "remember" has a feminine ending, "Julius" is read as two syllables, and "grasped" is pronounced "grasp'ed." All other lines are regular.

5. Phrase endings include "mind," line 2; "arrows" and "fortune," line 3; "arms" and "troubles," line 4; and "opposing," line 5. Lines 1–4 have feminine endings. Some actors like to break the rhythm with "that" in line 1. In line 4, "Or" breaks the rhythm.

6. Phrase endings are "age" and "hours," line 2; "play," line 5; and "anguish," line 6. "Come" and "age" break the rhythm. Elide "usual" to "us'al" and "torturing" to "tort'ring."

SKILL WORKSHEET 4

BREATHE ONLY AT THE PUNCTUATION MARKS

A. This is the example that was used in the text on page 95. Circle the breathing places (the punctuation marks), separate the phrases, and mark the stressed words. Underline those words that break the rhythm. Read the speech aloud, breathing only at the correct places.

Because of the Witches' prophesy that Banquo's children will be heirs to the throne, Macbeth, now King, contemplates killing Banquo.

> Macbeth: To be thus is nothing, but to be safely thus—
> Our fears in Banquo stick deep,
> And in his royalty of nature reigns that
> Which would be feared. 'Tis much he dares;
> And to that dauntless temper of his mind
> He hath a wisdom that doth guide his valour
> To act in safety. There is none but he
> Whose being I do fear; and under him
> My genius is rebuked, as it is said
> Mark Antony's was by Caesar.   (*Mac*, III, i)

B. Here are practice speeches. Circle the breathing places. Then practice reading the speeches aloud, breathing only at the correct places. Don't forget to identify the phrases, mark the stresses, and underline words that break the rhythm. Work out any necessary elisions.

1. Helena, frustrated because both Lysander and Demetrius profess love to her, speaks of Hermia in *A Midsummer Night's Dream*:

> Helena: Lo, she is one of this confederacy.
> Now I perceive they have conjoined all three
> To fashion this false sport in spite of me.   (III, ii)

2. The imprisoned King Richard II, overthrown by Bolingbroke and sensing his death, begins his famous monologue like this:

> Richard: I have been studying how I may compare
> This prison where I live unto the world;
> And, for because the world is populous,
> And here is not a creature but myself,
> I cannot do it. Yet I'll hammer it out.   (*RII*, v, i)

3. Prince Escalus condemns the riotous families after the Act I brawl in *Romeo and Juliet:*

Prince: What, ho! You men, you beasts,
          That quench the fire of your pernicious rage
          With purple fountains issuing from your veins!
          On pain of torture, from those bloody hands
          Throw your mistemp'red weapons to the ground
          And hear the sentence of your moved prince.   (I, i)

4. Here are Juliet's words as she paces and waits for the Nurse to bring news of Romeo.

Juliet: Give me my Romeo; and, when he shall die,
          Take him and cut him out in little stars,
          And he will make the face of heaven so fine
          That all the world will be in love with night
          And pay no worship to the garish sun.   (*Rom,* III, ii)

5. Brutus chastises Cassius for stealing from the poor to support his army in *Julius Caesar.* In this speech, practice speaking four lines on one breath.

Brutus: I did send to you
          For certain sums of gold, which you denied me;
          For I can raise no money by vile means.
          By heaven, I had rather coin my heart
          And drop my blood for drachmas than to wring
          From the hard hands of peasants their vile trash
          By any indirection.   (IV, iii)

TIPS AND ANSWERS FOR SKILL WORKSHEET 4

A. While this speech is a good breathing exercise, it is difficult to scan. You may or may not wish to work on the scansion. If you are leading a class through these exercises, you might assign it to some exceptional students and let them enjoy working it out.

      T'be thus / is noth / ing, but / t'be safe / ly thus—
      (You must elide each "to be" if you want ten syllables, although
      this line is often read effectively as twelve syllables.)

Our fears / in Ban / quo (silent beat) / <u>stick</u> deep (dee dum)
  *(A short line with a silent beat. A caesura would precede "stick,"
  which breaks the rhythm.)*
And in / his roy / al ty /of nat're (an extra syllable) / <u>reigns</u> that
  *(It does not hurt this line to have three syllables in the fourth root.
  "Reigns" breaks the rhythm. A caesura precedes "reigns.")*
Which would / be feared. / 'Tis much / he dares; / (dee dum)
  (Another short line.)
And to / that daunt / less tem / per of / his mind
He hath / a wis / dom that / doth guide / his val /our
  (A feminine ending.)
To act / in safe / ty. There / is none / but he
Whose be / ing I / do fear; / and un / der him
My gen' / us is / re buked, / as it / is said
  (Elide "genius" to "gen'us.")
Mark Ant / 'ny's was / by Caesar. (an extra syllable) / He chid /
  the sis / ters
  *(Elide "Antony's" to "Ant'ny's" The third foot has an extra syllable
  which does not hurt the line. The complete line has a feminine ending).*

Macbeth continues the line with "He chid the sisters" for a feminine ending. Phrase endings include "nature," line 3; "mind," line 5; "valour," line 6; "he," line 7; and "him," line 8.

B. 1. Lines 2 and 3 should be read with one breath. Scansion is like this:

<u>Lo</u>, she / is one / of this / con fed / 'ra cy.
  ("Lo" breaks the rhythm; elide "confederacy" to "confed'racy.")

Now I / per ceive / they have / con joined / all three
  (Some actors would emphasize both "all" and "three.")

To fash / ion this / <u>false</u> sport / in spite / of me.
  ("False" can break the rhythm.)

Phrase endings include "there," line 2, and "sport," line 3.

2. The first two lines should be read with one breath. Scansion is like this:

I have / been stud / y'ng how / I may / com pare
  ("Studying" is elided to two syllables.)

This pris / on where / I live / un to / the world;

And, for / be cause / the world / is pop / u lous,

And here / is not / a crea / ture but / my self,

I can / not do / it. Yet / I'll ham / mer't out.
(Elide "hammer it" to "ham mer't.")

Phrase endings include "studying" and "compare," line 1, and "live," line 2.

3. The previous line begins and completes the short line that opens this selection.

Will they / not hear? / What ho! / You men, / you beasts,

That quench / the fire / of your / per ni / cious rage

With pur / ple foun / tains is / su'ng from / your veins!
(Elide "issuing" to "issu'ng.")

On pain / of tor / ture, from / those blood / y hands

Throw your / mis temp / 'red weap / ons to / the ground
("Mistemp'red is already elided by the author.)

And hear / the sen / tence of / your mov / 'ed prince.
("Moved must be pronounced "mov'ed.")

Phrase endings include "fire" and "rage," line 2; "fountains," line 3; "hands," line 4; "ground," line 5; and "sentence," line 6.

4. The scansion is regular, except as indicated.

Give me / my Rom / 'yo; and, / when he / shall die,
(Here "Romeo" is spoken as two syllables, pronounced "Rom'yo.")

Take him / and cut / him out / in lit / tle stars,

And he / will make / the face / of heav'n / so fine
(Elide "heaven" to one syllable, "heav'n.")

˘　/　˘　/　˘　/　˘　/　˘　/
That all / the world / will be / in love / with night

˘　/　˘　/　˘　/　˘　/　˘　/
And pay / no wor / ship to / the gar / ish sun.

Phrase endings include "fine," line 3; "night," line 4; and "worship," line 5.

5. The scansion is regular, except as noted.

˘　/　˘　/　˘　/　˘　/　˘　/
Which I / re spect / not. I / did send / to you
(The end of the previous line begins this line.)

˘　/　˘　/　˘　/　˘　/　˘　/　(˘)
For cer / tain sums / of gold, / which you / de nied / me;
(Feminine ending.)

˘　/　˘　/　˘　/　˘　/　/　/
For I / can raise / no mon / ey by / vile means.

˘　/　˘　/　˘　/　˘　/　˘　/
By heav / en, I / had rath / er coin / my heart

˘　/　˘　/　˘　/　˘　/　˘　/
And drop / my blood / for drach / mas than / to wring

˘　˘　/　/　˘　/　˘　/　/　/
From the / hard hands / of peas / ants their / vile trash

˘　/　˘　/　˘　/　˘　/　˘　/
By an / y in / di rec / tion. I / did send
(The line that follows completes the thought.)

Phrase endings include "you," line 1; "money," line 3; "heart," line 4; "drachmas," line 5; and "peasants," line 6.

MORE ADVANCED STUDY: SKILL WORKSHEET 5

ANTITHESIS

According to Webster, "Antithesis is the placing of a sentence or one of its parts against another to which it is opposed to form a balanced contrast of ideas" (e.g., "Give me liberty or give me death"). Shakespeare frequently uses antithetical words, phrases, or thoughts, and you will be a better reader (or actor) of the language if you can identify them and allow the listener to hear them. For a more extended explanation of antithesis, see chapter 8.

Playing one antithetical word, phrase, or thought against another can be as simple as this example: "Rather than go to town, let's stay on the farm." When reading the line, play "go" against "stay," and "town" against "farm." Then, simultaneously play the entire first phrase, "Rather than go to town," against the second phrase, "let's stay on the farm," which is antithetical to it in thought. Read the line aloud a few times, and practice giving emphasis to the antithetical ideas.

A. Here are examples of antithesis in a Shakespearean speech.
  1. First, Brutus to Cassius in *Julius Caesar*:

Brutus:	What you have said	(1)
	I will consider; what you have to say	(2)
	I will with patience hear; and find a time	(3)
	Both meet to hear and answer such high things.	(4)
	Till then, my noble friend, chew upon this:	(5)
	Brutus had rather be a villager	(6)
	Than to repute himself a son of Rome	(7)
	Under these hard conditions as this time	(8)
	Is like to lay upon us.	(*JC*, 1, ii) (9)

Dig out the antithetical words, phrases, and thoughts in this speech, so you can play them against each other.

Now read the entire speech, and play the antithetical words or thoughts against each other. Notice how everything becomes clearer.

  2. In this next example, Romeo talks of love with his cousin, Benvolio, then notices that a street fight has taken place.

Benvolio:	Alas, that love, so gentle in his view,	(1)
	Should be so tyrannous and rough in proof!	(2)
Romeo:	Alas, that love, whose view is muffled still,	(3)
	Should without eyes see pathways to his will!	(4)

Where shall we dine? O me! What fray was here?	(5)
Yet tell me not, for I have heard it all.	(6)
Here's much to do with hate, but more with love:	(7)
Why, then, O brawling love! O loving hate!	(8)
O any thing, of nothing first create!	(9)
O heavy lightness! serious vanity!	(10)
Mis-shapen chaos of well-seeming forms!	(11)
Feather of lead, bright smoke, cold fire, sick health!	(12)
Still-waking sleep, that is not what it is!	(13)
This love feel I, that feel no love in this.	(14)
Dost thou not laugh?	(15)

Benvolio: No, cuz, I rather weep.   (*Rom*, I, i) (16)

Find the antithetical words, phrases or thoughts. Now read the speech aloud and play all the antithetical possibilities.

3. In *Richard II*, after having King Richard murdered, Bolingbroke, who will become the new king, condemns the killer, Exton.

Bolingbroke: They love not poison that do poison need,
              Nor do I thee. Though I did wish him dead,
              I hate the murderer, love him murdered.
              The guilt of conscience take thou for thy labor,
              But neither my good word nor princely favor.
              With Cain go wander through the shade of night,
              And never show thy head by day nor light.   (*RII*, v, vi)

Dig out the antithesis in this speech. Note the elision of "murderer" to "murd'rer" and the three syllables for "mur-der-'ed." (For line 6, I have used the *Folio*. The Pelican edition prefers "through shades of night.")

If you wish to work on the skill of digging out antithesis in more detail, use the complete book from which this worksheet is taken, and practice the many other examples to be found there.

ANSWERS AND TIPS FOR SKILL WORKSHEET 5

A. 1. Lines 1/2: "have said" is antithetical to "have to say"

Line 4: "hear" and "answer" are antithetical

Lines 3/4/5: "find a time/Both meet to hear and answer" (lines 3/4) is antithetical to "Till then . . . chew upon this" (line 5)

Lines 6/7: "a villager" and "son of Rome" are antithetical, as are "be" and "repute"

2. Line 1/2: "gentle in his view" and "tyrannous and rough in proof" are antithetical

Line 4: "without eyes" and "see pathways"

Line 6: "tell me not" and "have heard it all"

Line 7: "hate" and "love"

Line 8: "brawling" and "love," "loving" and "hate"

Line 9: "any thing" and "nothing"

Line 10: "heavy" and "lightness," "serious" and "vanity"

Line 11: "Mis-shapen chaos" and "well-meaning forms"

Line 12: All four phrases

Line 13: "still-waking" and "sleep," "is not" and "is"

Line 14: "love" and "no love"

Lines 15/16: "laugh" and "weep"

Also, the thought in line 13—"That's not what it [love] is" is antithetical to the type of "love" expressed in lines 7–12.

3. Line 1: The first phrase is antithetical to the second phrase—one might not love killing, but will do it anyway.

Line 2/3: "wish him dead" and "hate the murderer"—he had to die, but how could you kill such a fine king?

Line 3: "hate" and "love," "murderer" and "murdered"

Lines 4/5: "guilt of conscience" and "good word nor princely favor"— your reward for killing him is not my praise nor money, but guilt

Lines 6/7: "wander" and "show"—wander around, never show up here "shade of night" and "day nor light"—your existence is forever changed from light to darkness.

SKILL WORKSHEET 6

ELISION

Put simply, elision means either to shorten a word by omitting a vowel—as "int'rest" for "interest" or "virt'ous" for "virtuous"—or to combine two words into one by eliding a letter or letters—as "I'd" for "I had" or "I've" for "I have." Elision is used to shorten words, when necessary, so that fewer syllables are spoken to achieve the ten-syllable rhythm.

A. 1. Here are some examples.

Brutus: I had rather be a dog and bay the moon,   (*JC*, IV, iii)

The line has eleven syllables, and the rhythm is lost if you read the first foot "I had." Therefore, you elide "I had" to "I'd," and the first foot becomes "I'd rath." And the line scans like this:

$$\breve{}\,/\;\;\breve{}\,/\;\;\breve{}\,/\;\;\breve{}\,/\;\;\breve{}\,/$$
I'd rath / er be / a dog / and bay / the moon,

In an eleven or twelve-syllable line, before eliding, you must decide if the final syllable is a feminine ending. If it is not, then find the word or words to elide.

2. Here's another example of an eleven-syllable line.

Helena: Wherefore was I to this keen mockery born?   (*MND*, II, ii)

"Born" is obviously not a soft-ending word; it requires stress. Therefore, something has to be elided. Try eliding "mockery" (which has three syllables) to "mock'ry" (which has only two), and the rhythm works.

3. However, note this example from *The Merchant of Venice:*

Portia: The quality of mercy is not strained;
           It droppeth as the gentle rain from heaven
           Upon the place beneath.   (*MV,* IV, i)

In line 2, there are eleven syllables. But the "en" in "heaven" can be a feminine ending (the word is pronounced with stress on the first syllable), so the rhythm works without elision. You would not want to stress "en," as that would make the word sound very strange. Try it and see.

B. The next three examples are from *Twelfth Night*. Try this eleven-syllable line, and decide whether to elide one word or to have a feminine ending.

    1.

Captain: A virtuous maid, the daughter of a count.   (I, ii)

2. Here is an eleven-syllable line of the Duke. Choose between elision or a feminine ending.

Duke: I have unclasped
        To thee the book even of my secret soul.   (I, iv)

3. And here is Antonio's line to Sebastian—eleven syllables, same choice:

Antonio: To-morrow, sir; best first go see your lodging.   (III, iii)

(A hint: feminine endings are often "tion," "en," or "ing.")

For additional work, obtain the complete book from which this worksheet is taken, and begin on part one. If you become interested in the study of Shakespeare, you will find advanced work exciting and stimulating. It will turn on your brain and challenge your talent. Enjoy!

TIPS AND ANSWERS FOR SKILL WORKSHEET 6

B. 1. You must elide "virtuous" to "virt'ous," as "count" would not be a feminine ending.

2. You must elide "even" to "e'en," pronounced as one syllable and stressed.

3. The "ing" on "lodging" is not stressed, so it can be a feminine ending. Try saying "lodging" by stressing the "ing." That's probably not what you want!

CHAPTER 13

Scenes and Monologues

But when they ask you what it means, say you this;

HAMLET, IV, V

REFER TO YOUR complete collection of Shakespeare. While any edition
will do, some are more helpful than others. In this book, line notations are
taken from *The Pelican Shakespeare*, edited by Alfred Harbage (Viking Penguin, 1977). In other editions, lineation and punctuation may differ. The
punctuation in the Pelican edition is especially good. Check the scenes
and monologues listed in this chapter for the rehearsal material. All of
these will work with students. After selection, consider the following study
or rehearsal procedures.

Copy the scene. Then have the students type it themselves, double
spaced, and check it for spelling and punctuation accuracy. Have the students read the entire play aloud and know how this scene (or monologue)
fits into the overall action.

This study can be done in small groups comprised of those students
who are working on scenes or monologues from the same play. In a class of
twenty, you might use scenes and monologues from four plays; so each
reading/study group consists of five students.

Next, work out the scansion. Mark stressed syllables, mark feminine
endings or elide as necessary, and underline words that break the rhythm.
Circle all phrases and breathing points, and look up all words. If you have
time to uncover the antithesis, do that; it will add immeasurably to your
success. Only now are you ready to begin rehearsing the scene.

Scenes of two or three minutes in length (five minutes maximum) are enough for young actors—about forty to fifty lines, or twenty to twenty-five lines for each actor. To get fifty lines "right" is a challenging task, and allowing students to work on more than twenty-five lines each simply means that many more hours of rehearsal per scene are required. For monologues, twelve to fifteen lines are sufficient.

If you intend to present the scenes as an "evening of Shakespeare" or similar performance, short scenes and one-minute monologues work very well. For monologues, it's often helpful to use a second, nonspeaking actor standing downstage, giving the speaker someone to address. For soliloquies, the single actor can use the entire class as the audience. When performing, you might have someone other than the actors introduce the scenes, but have the actors introduce their own monologues.

The majority of scenes and monologues listed below are taken from the most "popular" eight plays, from which you probably select your curriculum. A few selections from other plays are also listed. Roles written for men can often be played by women.

SCENES AND MONOLOGUES FROM
THE EIGHT MOST POPULAR PLAYS

As You Like It

Scenes

- I, iii, lines 1–36, for two women (Celia and Rosalind), in prose. To continue, add one man (the Duke) for lines 37–85, for a section in verse. After the Duke exits, Celia and Rosalind have a verse scene from lines 86–134, which, in itself, makes a short scene.
- III, ii, lines 157–240, for two women (Celia and Rosalind), in prose.
- III, v, lines 1–137, for one man and two women (Silvius, Phebe and Rosalind—cut Celia and Corin), in verse. After Rosalind exits at line 79, there is a two-person verse scene between Phebe and Silvius.
- IV, iii, lines 76–181, for one man and two women (Oliver, who has most of the dialogue, Celia and Rosalind), mixes prose and verse.

Monologues

- II, vii, lines 139–166, for a man (Jaques), in verse.
- III, v, lines 35–63, for a woman (Rosalind), in verse.
- III, v, lines 108–134, for a woman (Phebe), in verse.
- Epilogue, a woman (Rosalind), in prose.

Hamlet

Scenes
- I, iii, lines 1–136, for two men and one woman (Laertes, Ophelia and Polonius), in verse.
- III, i, lines 88–161, for one man and one woman (Hamlet and Ophelia), mixed prose and verse.

Monologues
- I, iii, lines 10–44, for a man (Laertes), in verse.
- II, iii, lines 1–18, for a man (King), in verse.
- All acts, Hamlet's soliloquies, for men or women, in verse.

Henry V

Monologues
- Each act, Chorus soliloquies, for men or women, in verse.
- I, ii, lines 260–298, for a man (King), in verse.
- III, i, lines 1–34, for a man (King) in verse.
- IV, i, lines 216–270 (some cutting recommended), for a man (King), in verse.
- IV, i, lines 275–292, for a man (King), in verse.
- IV, ii, lines 15–37, for a man (Constable), in verse.
- IV, iii, lines 18–67, for a man (King), in verse.

Julius Caesar

Scenes
- I, ii, lines 25–177 (some cutting possible), for two men (Cassius and Brutus), in verse.
- II, i, lines 229–308, for one man and one woman (Portia and Brutus), in verse.
- IV, iii, lines 36–123, for two men (Brutus and Cassius), in verse. By cutting lines 124–143 and adding Lucius, the scene can continue with lines 144–162.

Monologues
- II, i, lines 10–34, for a man (Brutus), in verse.
- II, ii, lines 13–26, for one woman (Calphurnia), in verse.
- III, i, lines 254–275, for one man (Antony), in verse.

Macbeth

Scenes
- I, v, lines 1–70, and I, vii, lines 1–82, for one man and one woman (Macbeth and Lady Macbeth), in verse. Separate scenes or combine for one longer scene.

- II, ii, lines 1–73, for one man and one woman (Macbeth and Lady Macbeth) plus knocking sounds, in verse.
- III, i, lines 1–43, for two men (Macbeth and Banquo), in verse. Can continue as a scene for three men and a servant (Macbeth and Two Murderers and the servant), lines 44–144.

Monologues
- I, v, lines 36–52, for a woman (Lady Macbeth), in verse.
- I, vii, lines 1–28, for a man (Macbeth), in verse.
- III, i, lines 1–10, for a man (Banquo), in verse.

A Midsummer Night's Dream

Scenes
- II, i, lines 1–59, for one man and one woman (Puck and Fairy), in verse.
- II, i, lines 188–244, for one man and one woman (Demetrius and Helena), in verse.

Monologues
- I, i, lines 181–193, for a woman (Helena), in verse.
- I, i, lines 226–251, for a woman (Helena), in verse.
- II, i, lines 248–267, for a man (Oberon), in verse.
- III, ii, lines 6–34, for a man or a woman (Puck), in verse.
- III, ii, lines 145–161, for a woman (Helena), in verse.
- III, ii, lines 192–219, for a woman (Helena), in verse.
- III, ii, lines 254–277, for a man (Oberon), in verse.

Romeo and Juliet

Scenes
- I, i, lines 158–236 (cut as necessary), for two men (Romeo and Benvolio), in verse.
- II, ii, lines 1–138 or lines 139–190, or combine the two scenes, for one man and one woman (Romeo and Juliet), plus the off-stage voice of the Nurse and an off-stage noise, in verse.
- II, iii, lines 31–94, for two men (Friar and Romeo), in verse.
- II, iv, lines 152–202 or through line 204 if another character added, for one woman and one or two men (Nurse, Romeo and Peter), mixed prose and verse.
- II, v, lines 1–77, for two women (Juliet and the Nurse), in verse.
- III, ii, lines 1–143, for two women (Juliet and the Nurse), in verse.
- III, iii, lines 1–175 (cut some lines from the longer speeches), for two men and one woman (Friar, Romeo and Nurse), in verse.
- III, v, lines 65–126, for two women (Juliet and Lady Capulet), in verse.

By adding the Nurse and Capulet, the scene continues with lines 127–205; this is followed by a Juliet and Nurse scene, lines 206–244.

Monologues

- I, i, lines 79–101, for a man (Prince), in verse.
- I, iii, lines 17–48 (some cutting recommended), for a woman (Nurse), in verse.
- I, iii, lines 79–94, for a woman (Lady Capulet), in verse.
- I, iv, lines 53–94, for a man (Mercutio), in verse.
- II, i, lines 1–23, for a man (Romeo), in verse.
- III, ii, lines 1–34, for a woman (Juliet), in verse.
- III, ii, lines 97–127, for a woman (Juliet), in verse.

Twelfth Night

Scenes

- I, v, lines 133–297, for three women and one man (Malvolio, Olivia, Viola and Maria—Viola and Olivia have most of the lines), mixed prose and verse. Can begin at line 208 with Viola and Olivia; need a Malvolio for two lines.
- II, iv, lines 78–123, for one man and one woman (Viola [disguised as a man, Cesario] and the Duke), in verse.
- III, i, lines 91–176, for two women (Olivia and Viola), in verse.

Monologues

- II, ii, lines 16–40, for a woman (Viola), in verse.
- IV, iii, lines 1–21, for a man (Sebastian), in verse.
- V, i, lines 66–84, for a man (Antonio), in verse.

OTHER SELECTED SCENES AND MONOLOGUES

The Comedy of Errors

Scenes

- III, ii, lines 1–71, for one man and one woman (Antipholus of Syracuse and Luciana), in verse.
- IV, ii, lines 1–66, for two women and one man (Adriana, Luciana, Dromio of Syracuse), in verse.

Monologue

- V, i, lines 136–160, for one woman (Adriana), in verse.

The Taming of the Shrew

Scene

- II, i, lines 168–182, for one man and one woman (Petruchio and Kate), in verse.

Monologues
- IV, ii, lines 175–198, for a man (Petruchio), in verse.
- V, ii, lines 141–184, for a woman (Kate), in verse.

The Two Gentlemen of Verona

Scenes
- I, ii, lines 1–140, for two women (Julia and Lucetta), in verse.
- II, vii, lines 1–90, for two women (Julia and Lucetta), in verse.

Monologues
- II, iv, lines 189–211, for a man (Proteus), in verse.
- II, vi, lines 1–43, for man (Proteus), in verse.
- IV, iii, lines 11–36, for a woman (Silvia), in verse.

Love's Labor's Lost

Monologues
- III, i, lines 162–194, for a man (Berowne), in verse.
- V, ii, lines 89 –118, for a man (Boyet), in verse.
- V, ii, lines 779–802 for a woman (Princess), in verse.

The Merchant of Venice

Scene
- I, iii, lines 1–177 (or any section), for three men (Shylock, Bassanio and Antonio), in verse.

Monologue
- IV, i, lines 182–203, for a woman (Portia), in verse.

Much Ado About Nothing

Scenes
- III, i, lines 1–136, for four women (Hero, Beatrice, Ursula, and Margaret [one line]), in verse.
- IV, i, lines 253–328, for one man and one woman (Beatrice and Benedict), in prose.

All's Well That Ends Well

Scene
- I, iii, lines 130–249, for two women (Countess and Helena), in verse.

King Henry VI, Part 1

Monologue
- I, ii, lines 72–92, for a woman (Pucelle [Joan of Arc]), in verse.

King Henry VI, Part 2

Monologues
- I, i, lines 212–257, for a man (York), in verse.
- III, i, lines 4–41, for a woman (Queen Margaret), in verse.

King Henry VI, Part 3

Monologues
- II, v, lines 1–52, for a man (King), in verse.
- III, ii, lines 124–195 (with some cutting), for a man (Richard, Duke of Gloucester), in verse.

Richard III

Scene
- I, ii, lines 1–263 (use sections), for one man and one woman (Richard and Lady Anne) plus a few guards, in verse.

Monologues
- I, ii, lines 1–41, for a man (Richard), in verse.
- V, iii, lines 238–261, for a man (Richard), in verse.

King Henry IV, Part 1

Scene
- II, iii, lines 33–113, for one man and one woman (Hotspur and Lady Percy), in verse.

Monologue
- III, ii, lines 129–159, for a man (Prince Hal), in verse.

King Henry IV, Part 2

Monologue
- II, iii, lines 9–45, for a woman (Lady Percy), in verse.

Othello

Scenes
- III, iii, lines 93–257, for two men (Othello and Iago), in verse.
- IV, iii, lines 9–103 (with cutting), for two women; (Desdemona and Emilia), in verse.

Monologues
- I, iii, lines 377–398, for a man (Iago), in verse.
- II, i, lines 280–306, for a man (Iago), in verse.

King Lear
Monologues
- I, ii, lines 1–22, for a man (Edmund), in verse.
- II, iii, lines 1–21, for a man (Edgar), in verse.

Timon of Athens
Monologue
- IV, i, lines 1–41, for a man (Timon), in verse.

The Winter's Tale
Scene
- II, ii, lines 1–167, for one man and two women (Jailer, Emilia and Paulina), in verse.

Monologue
- III, ii, lines 90–115, for a woman (Hermione), in verse.

The Tempest
Scenes
- I, ii, lines 189–305, for one man and a second character who can be either a man or a woman (Prospero and Ariel), in verse.
- II, ii, lines 1–182, for three men (Caliban, Trinculo, and Stephano), mostly prose.
- III, i, lines 1–91, for one man and one woman (Miranda and Ferdinand), in verse.

Our revels now are ended.

THE TEMPEST, IV, i

PART THREE

For Professional Actors and Coaches: The One–Day Brush Up

I long to know the truth hereof at large.

THE COMEDY OF ERRORS, IV, iv

The Morning Session

Prepare thy battle early in the morning.
RICHARD III, V, iii

Y OU ARE A realistic actor. An opportunity arises to play Shakespeare, Molière, or another "classical" writer. You must read for the role. What do you do? How do you prepare this audition?

Here let us breathe
And haply institute a course of learning.
THE TAMING OF THE SHREW, I, i

EARLY CHARACTER CHOICES

Before beginning on the skills, here are some procedures to keep in mind. Try not to think about the character you plan to read. Shocking advice, I suppose. You want to dig out the subtext and the character choices and play those. But if you can wait on those choices, it will pay off handsomely.

Forcing a preconceived character, action, or method of "How one is supposed to play Shakespeare" on Shakespeare's language is one of the worst mistakes you can make. Forcing means you begin rehearsal knowing *how* you want to play the character *before* you have thoroughly mastered *what* the text is saying.

On the other hand, it is not forcing to have studied the text, perhaps seen a few productions of the play, and determined how you might play a specific role if given the opportunity. But be patient and, for the moment, forget "character." There are more important things to do first. We'll get to "character" later on.

Here are some of those "more important things":

- *When playing realism*, your job as an actor is to find your action and play it. Use a strong and clear voice, and play your action. "Play your action" refers to the things you do to achieve your objective.
- *When playing Shakespeare*, do the same thing. All you need to add are a few skills to handle the language. If playing realism is like walking, then playing Shakespeare is like dancing. You simply need to add a few "moves" to a process you already know and find the correct rhythm.

But it is also true that if you play Shakespeare without mastering these skills, your work will be as uninteresting and painful to the audience and your fellow actors as the ill-trained dancer is to the beholder and the partner.

This thought may be helpful: If you can hear the tune of a Beethoven sonata in your mind and you desire to pass this pleasure to the audience through the piano, your fingers must have the skills to play the notes. In playing Shakespeare, the skills you are about to learn are the composer's directions to you, like musical notations, and your voice is the instrument.

The four skills outlined below are as easy to learn as baseball and can be used at various levels of training and success. But to not use them is like playing baseball with your glove on the wrong hand. Not only does this blunder cause you to be a poor fielder, it also forces you to throw with the wrong arm. In both cases, you have crippled your own ability and won't be effective.

Little joy have I
To breathe this news; yet what I say is true.
RICHARD II, III, iv

Among other benefits, these skills will enable you to allow Shakespeare's language to be understood and heard clearly by the audience (or the director at your audition). Most American directors haven't spent much time analyzing Shakespeare's language. The directing jobs are elsewhere—for example, modern realistic plays, musicals, video, film—in a ratio of about 300:1. There is nothing that you, the actor, can do about this. When auditioning with Shakespeare, remember that casting agents and producers have even less background than directors, so let their lack of preparation motivate you to be vocally strong and very clear.

Or—not to crack the wind of the poor phrase.
HAMLET, I, iii

Regarding your voice, say what you mean, and say it loud and clear. Try to use your best voice—not some selected "character" voice. If saying what you mean involves subtext, use it. But don't indulge or rely on subtext when speaking Shakespeare, as problems (discussed in detail in part 1) will surely arise. And, strong voice or weak voice, don't waver from getting what you want from the person to whom you are speaking.

Another vocal clue: say what you think as you think it, and don't "reflect" on the thought before you speak. Don't think, then talk. Talk and think at the same time. Act on the words, not between the words. If you want to study this skill in more detail, refer to chapter 6 in part 1 of this book.

Above all, avoid asking, "How am I going to play this role?" If you speak clearly what you mean and pursue your intention in whatever way is necessary to achieve it, you will automatically discover a character. Let this discovery come to you through those actions.

Don't impose a character on this language. Rather, know the language, and you will discover the character who uses it. Be brave. Let the language guide you. It will show you "how" to play the role.

In summary, even if you know *how* you want to play a Shakespearean character, it won't help you one bit unless you know *what* the language is doing. Your character will be ineffective if what you are saying is unclear to the listener. At your audition, the director needs to hear if you can handle the language. Can you be understood? Are you believable?

We have to start here.

A double spirit
Of teaching and of learning instantly.
HENRY VI, PART 1, V, ii

FOUR BASIC SKILLS

If you use four basic skills, the director at your audition will listen to you and understand what you are saying. *These skills work, even if you don't understand what you're saying—as, perhaps, at a cold reading.*

The four skills are scansion, phrasing, end support, and breathing.

You might wonder about *analysis of text*, which won't receive much attention in this one-day lesson. But once the phrasing is correct, the actor will be very close to truthful line readings. Analysis also includes playing the antithetical words, phrases, or thoughts, which we will study. Complete chapters on antithesis and analysis are also included in the part 1 of this book.

You might also ask about *subtext*. When you set out to examine the emotional and psychological state of your character, it is difficult to ignore subtext. On the other hand, you can't really explore the character until you are certain what the character is doing. In Shakespeare, that action is discovered more through the text than the subtext. In this one-day lesson, we are concerned with the skills required to discover what the character is actually saying and doing. The actor can decide later what subtext, if any, is needed.

Think of Shakespeare's language this way:

Scan it • Break it up • Kick the box • Breathe!

FIRST NEW SKILL: SCANSION

So pause awhile . . .

To begin, select the passage or section that you are preparing for your audition, or sections of the play from which you will be reading. You are probably looking at blank verse. (If, by chance, you are reading a prose section—i.e., the language looks ordinary and without verse form—skip scansion and review the other three skills.) As you proceed, if you want more detailed explanations or examples for any definition or concept, the index will guide you to other sections of the book.

Blank verse is not poetry. It can be poetic, but in itself, it is merely a form of writing the English language. It was first used in the mid-sixteenth century and then perfected by Shakespeare and his contemporaries. It should not cause you any insecurity, because you actually speak blank verse all the time. ("Let's go to town and buy an ice cream cone" is blank verse!) A *regular* blank verse line consists of ten syllables, with a stress placed on every second syllable. The form is called iambic pentameter, with a rhythm that goes "dee dum dee dum dee dum dee dum dee dum."

This concept of "stresses" is valuable for actors, because it guides you to both the important words in the line and the author's intention. Marking the soft and stressed syllables in a blank verse line is called scanning the line, or scansion.

Let's do one. We'll break a line into "feet" of two syllables each for a total of five feet and ten syllables, then mark the stresses.

Let's go to town and buy an ice cream cone.

Break the line into feet:

Let's go / to town / and buy / an ice / cream cone.

Now mark the stresses: ∪ for unstressed, / for stressed.

∪　/　∪　/　∪　/　∪　/　∪　　/
Let's go / to town / and buy / an ice / cream cone.

Here's a better line from *Romeo and Juliet*:

Romeo:　　But soft! What light through yonder window breaks?　　(II, ii)*

But soft! / What light / through yon / der win / dow breaks?

∪　/　∪　/　　∪　　/　∪　/　∪　　/
But soft! / What light / through yon / der win / dow breaks?

When you read the line, place emphasis on the stressed syllables: "soft," "light," "yon," "win," "breaks." With your hand, beat out these stressed words or syllables on the table or chair. Read the line a few times by *beating out* and *over-stressing* the five stressed words or syllables. Then forget the scansion, and read the line naturally.

If you've beat out the rhythm with your hand and emphasized the stressed syllables, you will discover that when you "forget" scansion and read the line more naturally, you automatically give a slight emphasis to the stressed words. You will achieve naturalness and honesty, and do so by stressing the correct words.

For the Shakespearean line to be truthful, it is necessary to play the correct stresses. Let's test this idea by reading a line incorrectly. Here's the opening line from *The Merchant of Venice*:

Antonio:　　In sooth I know not why I am so sad.　　　　　　(I, i.)

∪　/　∪　/　∪　　/　∪　/　∪　/
In sooth / I know / not why / I am / so sad.

If we follow the scansion, the stresses are "sooth," "know," "why," "am," "sad." Read the line instead by stressing "In," "I," "not," "I," "so," and see what you get. That's probably not what you want for your audition!

---

*All Shakespeare quotations are taken from *The Complete Pelican Shakespeare*, Viking Penguin, 1977.

For anything so overdone is from the purpose of playing.

HAMLET, III, ii

So pause awhile . . .

Now you need a pencil, not a pen. Put this book down for thirty minutes, and select ten or twelve lines from your audition material. *Mark the scansion.* This will pay off handsomely later.

After marking the scansion on your ten or twelve lines, read them aloud a few times, hitting the stressed syllables. *Overdo it. Pound it out.* You can pull back to naturalism later. By overdoing, you discover meaning and "problems." Are there "problems?" Likely there are, so let's find them. For example, is there a stress that seems wrong? Or is there a line that won't scan to ten syllables? No, you're not miscounting, and, yes, trust your common sense. You've found an *irregular* line. Shakespeare obtains much of his effect by *inverting* stresses, which *changes* the rhythm of a line. Instead of "dee dum," a foot might be scanned "dum dee." He will also write *eleven-*syllable lines and, on some occasions, lines of twelve to fourteen syllables. On the following page are examples of these two variations.

So pause awhile . . .

Before continuing, if you need to brush up on the following terms, check the glossary or index for the following items:
- blank verse
- regular blank verse line
- feminine ending
- short or shared line
- rhymed couplet
- caesura
- elision
- iambic pentameter

Now we shall know some answer.

TITUS ANDRONICUS, III, iv

FIRST USUAL PROBLEM: SCANSION IS IRREGULAR

Here is an example from *A Midsummer Night's Dream*. (Refer to pages 19 and 102 for an example from *Romeo and Juliet*.)

Oberon: There sleeps Titania sometime of the night,
          Lulled in these flowers with dances and delight;
          And there the snake throws her enamelled skin,
          Weed wide enough to wrap a fairy in.   (II, i.)

Look at line 3. You may have one or more similar lines in your material.

And there / the snake / throws her / enam / elled skin,

Using *regular* scansion, in the third foot of the line, the word "throws" would not be stressed. The line would scan *incorrectly* like this:

And there / the snake / throws her / e nam / elled skin,

For the sense of the line, however, your common sense tells you that the verb "throws" is more important than the pronoun "her." And you are correct. So the third foot in the line is *irregular* and is called a trochee (pronounced tro' kee) or trochaic foot—which has the first syllable stressed and the second unstressed and scans like this:

And there / the snake / throws her / e nam / elled skin,

"Throws" is an action verb, and actors look for words like this. You would not want to leave it unstressed. This is a typical example of how Shakespeare changes the rhythm of the line and how you, as an actor, play "throws." In fact, for added emphasis, take a little sense pause just before you say it. That little pause is called a *caesura*—pronounced si-zhoor´-ə. It is not a breath pause, just a sense pause.

You discover changes in the rhythm by applying scansion and trusting your common sense. When rhythm changes, play it.

So pause a while . . .

Take fifteen minutes, and circle all words in your speech that break the rhythm.

It is not enough to speak, but to speak true.

MUCH ADO ABOUT NOTHING, V, i

_____

SECOND USUAL PROBLEM: TOO MANY SYLLABLES

Here is an example from *Hamlet*:

Hamlet:　To be, or not to be—that is the question:　　　　(III, i.)

To be, / or not / to be—/ that is / the ques / tion:

Here we have eleven syllables, with the eleventh ("tion") hanging on the end by itself. That syllable is called a *feminine ending*. It creates a soft ending, because in a regular blank verse line, the tenth and final syllable is stressed. Shakespeare uses the feminine ending frequently. You may have some feminine endings in the material you are preparing. Just let these lines end without placing stress on the final syllable. Feminine endings are often "tion," "ing," "eth," "er," and "en."

If you count eleven or twelve syllables in a blank verse line and note that the final syllable must be stressed, you cannot use the feminine ending. In this case, use *elision,* and contract two words or syllables into one— "I will" becomes "I'll." In the following line, Shakespeare has already elided a two-syllable words into one syllable to create an eleven-syllable line; but the actor must elide another word, as "man" is stressed and would not make a feminine ending.

Hamlet:　Horatio, thou art e'en as just a man.　　　　(*Ham,* III, ii)

Note "even" is already elided to "e'en" and pronounced as one syllable. The reader must elide "Horatio" to "Horat'o," pronounced as three syllables. Now the line can be spoken in ten syllables with correct rhythm.

Hor a / t'o, thou / art e'en / as just / a man.

So pause awhile …

That's a brief explanation of scansion. Before moving on to "break it up," be sure that you have clearly scanned the material you are preparing, marked the stresses, and circled all words that break the rhythm.

That matter is answered directly.

JULIUS CAESAR, III, iii

SECOND NEW SKILL: BREAK IT UP

We're talking about phrasing. According to Webster, a "phrase" may be a group of words that create a thought on which the mind can focus momentarily and which can be preceded or followed by a pause.

If you take any Shakespearean speech or sonnet, many of the phrases are separated by punctuation. Because it is easier to mark the phrases than it is to handle them vocally, you probably have some work to do before your audition.

In this example from *King Henry IV, Part 1*, many phrases are clearly marked by punctuation. Here the King demands that Prince Hal explain his unprincely behavior. (See page 27 for another example from *Julius Caesar*.)

King:	Lords, give us leave: the Prince of Wales and I	(1)
	Must have some private conference; but be near at hand,	(2)
	For we shall presently have need of you. *(They exit.)*	(3)
	I know not whether God will have it so	(4)
	For some displeasing service I have done;	(5)
	That, in his secret doom, out of my blood	(6)
	He'll breed revengement and a scourge for me;	(7)
	But thou dost in thy passages of life	(8)
	Make me believe that thou art only marked	(9)
	For the hot vengeance and the rod of heaven	(10)
	To punish my misreadings. Tell me else,	(11)
	Could such inordinate and low desires,	(12)
	Such poor, such bare, such lewd, such mean attempts,	(13)
	Such barren pleasures, rude society,	(14)
	As thou art matched withal and grafted to,	(15)
	Accompany the greatness of thy blood	(16)
	And hold their level with thy princely heart?	(III, ii) (17)

In lines 8–11, there are phrases not separated by punctuation, but notice how many are easily identified.

What about phrases that aren't defined by punctuation? Here are lines 4–11 with caesuras (//) inserted to mark the phrases. (Some actors prefer to circle phrases.)

King:	I know not whether God will have it so //	(4)
	For some displeasing service // I have done;	(5)
	That, in his secret doom, out of my blood //	(6)
	He'll breed revengement // and a scourge for me;	(7)
	But thou dost // in thy passages of life //	(8)
	Make me believe // that thou art only marked //	(9)
	For the hot vengeance // and the rod of heaven //	(10)
	To punish my misreadings. Tell me else, *(etc.)*	(11)

Why bother to mark the phrases? Your goal is to know the phrasing of the line so that you can (1) separate the thoughts, (2) play one phrase against another, (3) allow a thought to continue to the next line, as needed, and (4) identify your breathing spots, just like singing.

The caesuras are inserted only to mark the phrasing for rehearsal purposes. Once your phrasing is clear, remove most of the pauses, and speak from breathing point to breathing point. You don't want to impose pauses similar to those in realistic dialogue on the rhythm of blank verse. That technique simply makes your acting indulgent. Use non-breathing-point pauses only when they are absolutely necessary for clarity.

So pause awhile . . .

Take fifteen minutes, and circle or mark the phrases in your material. You should already have marked the scansion and circled the words that break the rhythm. Pause here before you continue to "antithesis."

END MORNING SESSION: LUNCH TIME

You have deserved
High commendation, true applause, and love.

AS YOU LIKE IT, I, ii

USEFUL IDEAS TO REMEMBER:

CHAPTER 15

The Afternoon Session

Thus did he answer me, yet said
I might know more hereafter.
CYMBELINE, IV, ii

———

As you probably know, placing one idea against another is called *antithesis*. Shakespeare uses antithetical words, phrases, or thoughts in nearly every speech. Having the skill to discover and play antithesis is a key to handling Shakespeare's language. For the actor, antithetical words, phrases, or thoughts provide clear insight into the meaning of Shakespeare's text.

ANTITHESIS

To have my praise for this, perform a part
Thou hast not done before.
CORIOLANUS, III, ii

———

Antithesis is a noun meaning contrast or direct opposite. Placing one antithetical word, phrase, or thought against another can be as simple as this example: "Rather than go to town, let's stay on the farm." When reading the line, play (give equal emphasis to) "go" against "stay" and "town" against "farm." Then, simultaneously play the entire first phrase, "rather than go to town," against the second phrase, "let's stay on the farm," which is antithetical to it in thought. You should immediately hear a new clarity in the sentence.

From Brutus' speech on page 27, let's dig out some antithetical words, phrases, and thoughts so we can play them against each other.

Lines 1/2: "do love me" is antithetical to "would work me to." Read the lines aloud, and play these two phrases against each other.

Lines 3/4: the phrase "How I have thought of this" (in the past) is antithetical to the phrase "shall recount hereafter" (in the future). Read the lines aloud, and play these thoughts against each other.

Lines 6/7: "have said" is antithetical to "have to say."

Lines 8/9: "find a time/Both meet to hear and answer" is antithetical to line 10: "Till then . . . chew upon this:"

Line 9: "hear" and "answer" are antithetical.

Lines 11/12: "a villager" and "son of Rome" are antithetical, as are "be" and "repute."

In a larger sense, the *thought* in lines 1–the middle of line 3 is antithetical to the *thought* in lines 3^1/$_2$–5^1/$_2$. The first thought is pretty much "I hear and understand what you're saying to me; I've also thought about this and will discuss it later." The next thought is "right now I need more time to think, so stop speaking." The idea of "listening to you" followed by "now I don't want to listen to you" is antithetical. You need to set up the first thought, so that you can play against it when you speak the antithetical thought.

Read the first four lines aloud, playing the antithetical words and phrases we've noted, and then play the entire thought of those four lines against the entire thought of the next three. As an actor, you must discover and play these textual clues to clearly reveal what the character is saying.

Now read the entire speech, and play the antithetical words and thoughts against each other. Notice how everything becomes clearer. Practice this example, and you will discover that you are speaking Brutus's words with confidence and understanding. Notice that your work is *specific* rather than *generalized.*

So pause awhile . . .

Take one hour, and dig out the antithetical words, phrases, and thoughts in your material. It works best to have a small group of actors do this together. When it comes to digging out antithesis, four or five brains are better than one. Assemble a group, make some coffee, and plunge in.

Digging out antithesis is—horrors—part of analysis! Many actors, especially when young, hate analysis. These actors prefer to trust their "natural talent," or the director, to guide them to line meanings; or they prefer to discover meaning through action. They hate to "talk about meaning" and are often concerned that too much text study will kill spontaneity.

That attitude is somewhat understandable. With realistic text, you can often discover what a line means by reading it clearly, listening, and playing your action.

However, when using the "discovery-through-action" approach, you will have more success with realism than with heightened text. The reason is simple: Blank verse has a defined structure. This is not to undervalue modern text—good writers always have a language structure—but to clarify blank verse.

When working with blank verse, before committing to an action, you must be certain what the verse is doing. If you select your action before you recognize the stresses, or before you clearly see the antithetical words and thoughts, or before you know which words break the rhythm, you can rehearse for weeks and never once read the line with its best possibilities. You can play your action and listen intently to everything said to you, but if you don't know what the language is doing, your work will remain unfinished. This failure is not a reflection on talent, but on lack of practice or coaching with blank verse.

We that have good wits have much to answer for.

AS YOU LIKE IT, V, i

When working with blank verse, actors who neglect to mark phrasing, find the antithesis, and analyze what the line is doing often "lock in" on a reading and won't budge from that comfort zone. These actors are usually making "character choices" before completing text analysis. The actor may fall back on the idea that "this is how my character would say it."

These actors will cling to an interpretation until the director forces them to try other approaches. Now the work tends to become artificial. The director is no longer suggesting that the actor try other actions, but is bogged down trying to dislodge rote or emotional indulgence.

Text study must precede character analysis. The defense that "this is how my character would say it" may or may not be supported by what the line is actually doing. The response may simply be the actor's easy way out of uncovering those possibilities.

As with selecting actions, it follows that you need to know everything the language is doing before you select a character. If not, your selection may be entirely out of sync with the author's meaning, and you end up trying to force the language to fit the character choice. On the other hand, if you develop your character after you are certain of the text, you will find that the words are exactly what your character needs to achieve the action.

What if you have a director who forces a character choice on you before you are completely certain what the language is doing? This is a serious problem, usually caused by the actor not doing the necessary prerehearsal homework. To avoid this situation, always complete text analysis before you begin rehearsals. Should there be an emergency where you are thrust into a role that is written in blank verse, get some help, and pull a few all-nighters completing your text analysis. Then determine if the director's choices fit the text in a meaningful way that you can play. If you disagree, at least you now have a solid knowledge of the text to support your view and can perhaps win over the director to another choice.

Regarding accents that may be required for some characters, or may be a director's concept, do your complete text analysis first, then slowly add the accent one word or one line at a time. Keep within your truthful sense of the language, and simply allow it to be pronounced differently.

For a funny, yet moving example of a director forcing a preconceived character on an actor, see Neil Simon's film, *The Goodbye Girl*, in which Richard Dreyfuss is required to play Richard III the director's way.

Of course, you can technically perform an action without knowing what you are saying, i.e., you understand only the general sense of a scene or moment but have not researched thoroughly the possibilities within your own lines. For example, in Act IV of *The Merchant of Venice*, Portia is trying to persuade (her action is "to persuade") Shylock not to take his "pound of flesh." Her action is properly connected to the other character, and its effectiveness can only be measured in terms of the other's response.

Portia:	I pray you, let me look upon the bond.
Shylock:	Here 'tis, most reverend Doctor, here it is.
Portia:	Shylock, there's thrice thy money off'red thee.
Shylock:	An oath, an oath! I have an oath in heaven: (iv, i.)

You can speak the lines, play your action, and make it convincing. You can get by without knowing what the choices are for the line "Shylock, there's thrice thy money offer'd thee." *But if you do know what the choices are, something more than "to persuade" happens as you play your action.*

Let's assume that you have marked the scansion, worked out the phrasing, tested the antithetical possibilities, and have concluded that there are at least four possible approaches to this line. What you select, of course, will influence how you eventually decide to play the character:

1. No choice. Just read the line, and let the audience decide what it means.

2. Emphasize the amount of money Shylock will receive by foregoing the bond.
3. Read the bond (the prop), then lose patience with his inflexible position.
4. Confidentially urge him, speaking as a neutral legal authority, to make the more merciful choice.

Selecting number four, for example, guides you to read the line differently (although still "to persuade") than if you had selected number three. Of course, your final selection in performance is based somewhat on how Shylock hands you the bond and his intent with "Here 'tis, most reverend doctor, here it is." But you now have a range of choices from which you can respond, and you have both a mental and a vocal familiarity with the possibilities. That's the position you want to be in during performance. You don't want to be locked in to a specific reading of the line because it "feels good" or "is how my character would say it."

The audience will know what you're saying when you know what you're saying. Character choices made after text study allow character and language to work harmoniously. Know clearly what you are saying, then know your action. This knowledge will lead you to character.

I understand thee, and can speak thy tongue.
ALL'S WELL THAT ENDS WELL, IV, i

Here are more difficult lines, which become clear and easy to speak if you analyze them and handle the phrases according to your discoveries:

Sonnet 27

Weary with toil, I haste me to my bed,	(1)
The dear repose for limbs with travel tired;	(2)
But then begins a journey in my head,	(3)
To work my mind, when body's work's expired:	(4)

Read the lines through once, then let the following discoveries (the analysis) help clarify your reading.

1. In line 1, the first and fourth syllables are stressed, not the second and fourth. The first foot is a trochee.
2. In line 1, antithetical words include "weary" and "haste," and also "toil" and "bed."
3. In line 1, "I haste me to my bed" can be two phrases, if you don't overdo it, and that allows you to make something of "haste."

4. In line 1, support "bed." Don't play the pronouns "my," "me," or "I." *Never play pronouns, unless by deliberate choice called for by the action.*

5. Line 2 is a regular line, but use three phrases, so you can be clear on "travel tired."

6. In line 3, "But" turns the thought around, but need not necessarily be stressed; the line can be a regular line.

7. Line 3 is antithetical to line 1.

8. In line 3, "begins a journey" is antithetical to "travel tired."

9. In lines 2/3, "head" is antithetical to "limbs."

10. In line 4, "To work my mind" is antithetical to "when body's work's expired."

11. In line 4, "mind" is antithetical to "body."

Read the lines again, playing the antithesis. Notice the difference. These clues have guided you to Shakespeare's meaning through the blank verse structure. Very little modern realism is structured this way, and that is why, with Shakespeare, you must start with the language and know what it offers. Then, if you are clear about the actions you've discovered through the language, your character will take care of itself. Later, in rehearsal, you can develop your character to the full extent of your ability. You will find, if you haven't already, that Shakespeare's language is so good, it actually helps you to achieve your objective.

Actors with limited skills, complete beginners, "personalities," and inexperienced acting teachers or directors often work "in reverse." When approaching a script, they first decide "how" to play a character, then proceed to make the action and line readings fit the character choice.

This reverse approach can sometimes be successful with modern realistic dialogue, especially on film, but it never works with heightened text. You can't play a "personality" here. You must deal with the language, because the language dominates. With Shakespeare, the "character first" approach will fail every time.

Antithesis is such a key to discovering Shakespeare's text that a complete chapter is devoted to it in part one. After you finish the one-day lesson, if you have time to study one more thing, make it antithesis.

PHRASING EXERCISE

So pause awhile ...

In this phrasing exercise, the actor speaks the language from thought to thought and must deal with each thought individually, not running them together unless by choice. Take the next hour, and do the exercise with the material you are preparing.

Set two objects apart from each other. The objects can be chalkboards, chairs, books, people, trees, it doesn't matter. The distance can be four feet or much more, as you will discover, but you may want to begin with the objects about six feet apart. Stand by one of the objects. Begin your lines. At each punctuation point, pause and cross to the other object (location), then resume. Breathe as you cross, then speak the next line from the next object, until you come to another punctuation point—pause— cross while breathing—speak, etc. You can go around a room like this, speaking thought to thought, from object to object.

The exercise forces you to recognize how the lines are broken into thoughts and how the thoughts must be separated; allows you to use all the air you wish to use on individual phrases; allows you to breathe in while walking to the next object; allows you to prepare the next line while breathing in and moving; and allows you to speak after you've filled your lungs— which you have plenty of time to do while moving to the next object.

In this exercise, you are forced to deal with each phrase individually and can't rush, because you must stop speaking to move and breathe at each punctuation point. This exercise always works.

The exercise can be simplified and practiced in two parts. First, do the exercise, but don't worry about the breathing. Just concentrate on separating the phrases, which you must do to accomplish the exercise. Once you feel comfortable with the separation of phrases, add the concentration on breathing correctly. With practice, you will find a wonderful rhythm: line and breath out, walk and breathe in, line and breath out, walk and breathe in, etc. Ultimately, you should have your objects only four or five feet apart so that you only take one breath in while walking, and fill your lungs completely each time.

Now take the next hour and review all antithetical words, phrases, or thoughts in your ten or twelve lines of material. Practice playing the ideas against each other. Also, do the phrasing exercise while adding concentration on the antithetical ideas and other scansion discoveries.

You now have the basic skills to act your lines from phrase to phrase, which means from thought to thought, and this is exactly what you want to do.

END AFTERNOON SESSION

Have dinner now, and rest your brain.

When my cue comes, call me and I will answer.
A MIDSUMMER NIGHT'S DREAM, IV, i

———————

CHAPTER 16

The Evening Session

If you be not too much cloyed with fat meat,
our humble author will continue the story.

HENRY IV, PART 2, EPILOGUE

Now that we have scanned the lines, found the antithesis, and separated the phrases, our concentration will be on speaking those phrases so that the listener knows exactly what you are saying. A major clue is the realization that in a phrase or verse line, the final word is often the most important.

THIRD NEW SKILL: KICK THE BOX

"Kick the box" means to support the final syllable of the verse line. When you support the final syllable or word, you allow the thought expressed in the line to "continue." The thought doesn't just end, as it does if you ease off on the final word or run out of breath and lose the word.

If you want your Shakespeare to work, you need to develop the skill required to support the final word and thought in each line.

AN ASIDE

Once you have learned this skill, apply it to all text. You may be amazed to discover how frequently the final word or phrase is the most important part of a prose line. Modern writers are not writing blank verse or placing a stress on the tenth syllable of their line, but the idea of supporting the entire second part of the prose line, if not the last word, will almost always work for you. Examples from George Bernard Shaw, Arthur Miller, and Shakespeare are included in chapter 4.

Supporting the last word of the verse line is not easy. Physiologically, our diaphragm doesn't want to work that way. The muscle is "lazy" and prefers relaxation to tension.

During voice training, actors learn to use the diaphragm to support speech. But even after training, many actors forget to "kick the box." They forget for three reasons:

- The effort to read the line "naturally" and truthfully encourages us to fade out at the end
- We don't practice speaking blank verse on a daily basis
- Breath support becomes lackadaisical, and rather than support the ends of lines, it is easier to allow them to fade away as they do in our daily speech

Because our vocal muscles are uncomfortable with a change, any effort to support the ends of lines will seem strange at first and perhaps "overdone." But supporting is correct. If you don't support the end of the verse line, one can project that your Shakespeare will not be clear or truthful. The listener won't quite know what you are saying.

You need great physical energy to speak Shakespeare's verse, and kicking the box helps you to remember to use your body. Energy is a key to your success. Remember, Shakespeare's plays were written to be performed

- Outdoors
- In broad daylight
- For large audiences
- With much of the audience standing for the entire play
- With people sitting on stage
- Amid concession sales like a baseball game
- With birds flying around
- With the audience probably talking back to the actors

If you try speaking in that setting, you will discover immediately how much vocal energy is required.

THE KICK-BOX EXERCISE

So pause awhile . . .

In this example, Romeo is speaking to Friar Laurence:

Romeo: Thou canst not speak of that thou dost not feel.   (iii, iii.)

Scan the line. Now speak the line in a "natural" way, allowing the final word "feel" to fade away. What is the line about?

Now circle the word "feel." Then place a small cardboard box on the floor and stand by it. Speak the line, and when you get to "feel," kick the box. Don't kick on "not," and don't kick after "feel." Kick right on the *f* of the word.

It may help if you take just a split-second pause (a caesura) before "feel," as this allows you to position yourself (and the word) and to get your leg and balance ready to kick—then kick. Later, forget the pause, which is only for the exercise.

You will notice that the kick does two things—it gets your body physically involved in speaking the language, and it gets you to support the word "feel." The intent here is not to overplay "feel." You don't want to shout it or call great attention to it. You simply support it, as opposed to letting it fade out. Your ear should tell you that the line means different things when you support or don't support "feel."

If you don't support "feel," Romeo seems to be telling the Friar not to "speak of things." That information is in the first half of the line.

If you do support "feel," Romeo may be reminding the Friar that he is celibate and has never felt the love of a woman, therefore how can he advise? That reading gives both actors much more to work with. Try it.

There are other interpretations of this line, but you should see immediately the difference between supporting and not supporting the final word. Not supporting makes the line a "general" comment—supporting makes it "specific." Remember Stanislavski's famous observation: *"In general is the enemy of art".*

Let's look at two other examples, as one of these may be similar to the material you are preparing. In the first line of *Romeo and Juliet*, the final word has more than one syllable.

Chorus: Two households, both alike in dignity,   (i, Pro)

Kick on "ty," not on "dig" or "ni"—because "ty" is the tenth syllable. Again, don't smash it like the box, just support it. If you kick on "dig" (the second syllable of the fourth foot), you will notice that "nity" falls off. Try it.

Remember feminine endings? If the line scans to eleven syllables, you support number ten, not number eleven. With a feminine-ending line, let the last syllable be soft. On "To be, or not to be—that is the question," kick on "ques," and let "tion" be soft.

Here's Portia to Shylock in *The Merchant of Venice* (a line with a feminine ending).

| Portia: | It droppeth as the gentle rain from heaven | (IV, i.) |

Kick on "heav" and let "en" be soft.
But here's Shylock to the Duke in the same play:

| Shylock: | I have possessed your Grace of what I purpose, | (IV, i.) |

This line has a feminine ending, and you kick on "pur." However, as an actor choice, you might also support "pose" for the added threat implied. Try it both ways.

Trust your common sense. If you find that the last word in a specific line doesn't merit stress, pull back. Don't hit it so hard. Make it real. After you've worked the exercise, forget it—but remember to always kick the box.

Don't take it to the audition with you, and don't take it to a performance. This is a rehearsal exercise designed to help you support the thought all the way through a verse line. It's not academic; the exercise leads to a skill that you will automatically apply to blank verse lines from now on. As with all acting, play the moment, don't try to remember what you rehearsed.

Read these next four lines in a "natural" way, allowing the final words in each line to *fade away* so you can barely hear them.

Sonnet 35
No more be grieved at that which thou hast done:
Roses have thorns, and silver fountains mud;
Clouds and eclipses stain both moon and sun,
And loathsome canker lives in sweetest bud.

Now read the lines again, this time supporting the last words (kicking the box). Notice how the thoughts in the lines continue from line to line when you support the endings. You also allow our ears to enjoy the pleasure of the rhyme!

So pause awhile . . .

Take the next hour, and do this exercise with every line in your material. Practice supporting the final words, then the final phrases. Trust your ear. As with some of the other exercises, this one is most enjoyable if you assemble a small group and take turns reading the lines. Hearing others read your material can be very rewarding.

You've just become a great deal better at reading Shakespeare!

> *I do believe that these applauses are*
> *For some new honors . . .*
> JULIUS CAESAR, I, ii

Now, can you scan it, phrase it, support it, and still breathe? Sure!

REVISITING A FAMILIAR SKILL: BREATHE!

It's absurd for an actor to run out of breath, and doing so can destroy a fine characterization. Even worse, it also destroys the author's line. Tyrone Guthrie liked to say that any well-trained actor could speak seven lines of blank verse on one breath, in a large theatre, with clear diction, and without rushing (*On Acting*, 14). It may take you some time to master that skill, and you won't need it for your audition, but you do need to breathe correctly, even if you can't speak seven lines on one breath.

When do you breathe? It's easy to decide with Shakespeare, but it's harder to discipline yourself to do it. Breathe at the natural stops, which are identified by punctuation marks.

Look at these lines, in which the Friar advises Juliet how to use the sleeping potion. (See page 45 for another example from *Macbeth*.)

Friar:	To-morrow night look that thou lie alone;	(1)
	Let not the nurse lie with thee in thy chamber.	(2)
	Take thou this vial, being then in bed,	(3)
	And this distilling liquor drink thou off;	(4)
	When presently through all thy veins shall run	(5)
	A cold and drowsy humor; for no pulse	(6)
	Shall keep his native progress, but surcease;	(7)
	No warmth, no breath, shall testify thou livest;	(8)
	The roses in thy lips and cheeks shall fade	(9)
	To wanny ashes, thy eyes' windows fall	(10)
	Like death when he shuts up the day of life;	(*Rom*, IV, i) (11)

As clearly as we can tell, this speech has typical Shakespearean punctuation. We must remember that our versions of the plays were taken from actors' scripts, and the punctuation has been "studied and worked" for four hundred years by scholars. Different editions of the plays change the punctuation slightly.

The breathing points are the punctuation marks. Circle them, then read the speech and breathe at each mark. You will find that it is quite easy to speak from one breathing point to the next. The longest stretch is one and one-half lines.

Don't breathe after "run" in line 5 or "pulse" in line 6. But try it once to discover the problem. You will see immediately that the choice is wrong. Your common sense and good ear will tell you.

Don't breathe at the end of a verse line simply because it is the end of the line on paper. Unless there is punctuation, it isn't the end of the phrase or thought. Many verse lines are enjambed, which means the thought in one line continues to another line without separation by punctuation. In the Friar's speech, lines 5, 6, 9, and 10 are enjambed. Breathe at the end of a verse line only if there is punctuation, as in lines 1, 2, 3, 4, 7, 8, and 11.

Read these four lines, which have numerous punctuation points, and breathe at each natural stop (all of the punctuation points). Ariel, a spirit, greets his master, Prospero, who has sent for him in *The Tempest:*

Ariel:	All hail, great master! Grave sir, hail! I come	(1)
	To answer thy best pleasure; be't to fly,	(2)
	To swim, to dive into the fire, to ride	(3)
	On the curled clouds. To thy strong bidding task	(4)
	Ariel and all his quality.	(1, ii.) (5)

Did you cheat? Read it a second time, *and make yourself breathe at all punctuation points.* You will find that you don't need that many breaths. You may be able to read the first line breathing only after "master" and the second "hail," cutting two breaths. But don't cut them unless you don't need them. You probably would have used the breaths in the three-thousand seat original Globe Theatre, but won't use them in the audition space, small theatres, or film.

If you breathe after "fly," "swim," and "fire," it may help you create images with each phrase, which would be appropriate for the character.

Trust your judgment. Your goal is to have a reserve of breath power available at all times and to be able to kick the box on the final word of a sentence. If you haven't enough breath left to support the final word, you are not breathing correctly. Inserting more breaths into the lines is not the best solution (although it is one), because these added breaths break up the verse line in an unnatural way, and this will likely leave you gasping and unclear.

Portia: The quality of mercy is [*breathe*] not strained;   (*MV*, IV, i.)

If you read the line that way, you are the one who is strained!
On the other hand, the phrasing in most blank verse lines can be separated at least once by inserting a caesura. The caesura, however, is not usually a breathing place.

The quality of mercy // [*caesura sense break*] is not strained;

If you need to insert a breath, do it where the phrasing allows and where it will add emphasis to what you just said or are about to say. But in the above line, you obviously don't need a breath. "Strained" might be emphasized by preceding it with a caesura, but not a breath.

However, try reading the line by pausing to breathe (or emote, or "act") after "quality," "mercy," and "not." If this sounds right to you, postpone your audition for a day. Go back to the top of this "One-Day Brush Up" and start over. You've missed the point!

Your goal is to breathe correctly—to fill your lungs at each breathing point—and to avoid little gasping breaths that fill only one-third of your lung capacity. Take the time to breathe deeply, then speak the line on the exhale. The words ride on the air; just send them out.

Yet words do well
When he that speaks them pleases those that hear.
AS YOU LIKE IT, III, V

Actors accustomed to realistic text often want to "enhance" that text with sounds, gasps, crying, whispering, pauses for effect, sighs, and "ahs." With heightened text, such "enhancements" tend to destroy the rhythm of the language. When the rhythm is lost, usually the antithetical ideas are lost. When the antithetical ideas are lost, the audience listens only passively, because they are not quite certain what you are saying.

For an excellent example of reading heightened text with great heart and commitment, correct breathing, and without breaking the rhythm with unnecessary pauses or character "enhancements," watch Kenneth Branagh speak the Saint Crispin's speech in Act IV of his film, *Henry V*. It's perfection. Other similar examples are listed in part 4.

You can rant and rave with a powerful voice and great energy, but the audience will listen only passively if they don't know exactly what you are saying.

Embellishing the language with emotion for the reason that "my character would do this" will usually not work for you in Shakespeare. Your performance becomes indulgent, because you've lost *what* is being said in favor of *how* it is being said.

Generally this direction works: If you need to cry, cry after the line, not on the line. Reason? We must hear the words first, then we can experience your sorrow without the irritation caused by a muffled line. If you must whisper, do it so that everyone, including the back row, can hear and understand clearly. Again, you risk the irritation caused by the muffled line.

There is more on this subject in part 1 of this book, but for your audition, forget "pregnant pauses" for emotional effect. Keep the language moving, keep the rhythm, and pause to breathe at the correct points. The emotion, you will discover, is already written into the text. You need only find it and play it honestly.

So pause awhile . . .

Here is a good rehearsal exercise. Clearly mark the breathing points in your material. Then read your speech aloud, and use up all of your air on each group of words, from breathing point to breathing point. Make certain that you support the final words, but otherwise empty your lungs between breathing points.

This exercise allows you to discover how much force and power you have available. It also implants in your mind the necessity to breathe. Use all of the air between each breathing point, even if the line has only one word. *Do it now.*

As you practice the exercise, you will begin to notice that taking the breath gives you the split second you need to grasp your next line. As you inhale physically, you also inhale mentally, so to speak, and grab the next line. Then out it comes on the next breath.

If it is your tendency as an actor to break up lines with "embellishments" for emotional effect, this exercise may show you that the only pauses you really need in Shakespeare are the breathing points. Keep the phrases intact, the words moving, and play the antithetical ideas against each other.

You will discover that application of too much emotion to heightened text does nothing but bury the meaning, and the audience stops listening.

Don't get ahead of yourself by thinking ahead. As with all good acting, stay in the moment, listen, and respond. Don't anticipate or indicate. Realize that after you speak a line, your breathing skill allows you to mentally secure your next line, and this skill will help you develop the confidence you need to stay in the moment.

If you have three or four lines with no breathing points, try to conquer them. You will need a deep breath before you start line one and will need to control the release of your air as you speak the lines, or you'll never make it through and surely won't have anything left for the important final word. If you can't yet handle three or four lines, find an appropriate place to insert your breath—but hopefully no more than one. Then begin a walking or jogging program and build up your breath support!

Try this example. In *Henry V*, the Bishop of Canterbury tells the King that if he will attack France, the Church will supply him with the money needed for the war.

Canterbury:	O, let their bodies follow, my dear liege,	(1)
	With blood, and sword, and fire to win your right!	(2)
	In aid whereof we of the spiritualty	(3)
	Will raise your highness such a mighty sum	(4)
	As never did the clergy at one time	(5)
	Bring in to any of your ancestors.	(1, ii.) (6)

Read the speech aloud, and see if you can do lines 3 through 6 without a breath. If you can't make it, take a breath after "sum," but notice that the speech flows better without the breath. Note, too, that "spiritualty" must be elided from four to three syllables—spir't'ual ty.

Here are seven lines Chorus speaks before Act IV of *Henry V*:

Chorus:	Now entertain conjecture of a time	(1)
	When creeping murmur and the poring dark	(2)
	Fills the wide vessel of the universe.	(3)
	From camp to camp, through the foul womb of night,	(4)
	The hum of either army stilly sounds,	(5)
	That the fixed sentinels almost receive	(6)
	The secret whispers of each other's watch.	(iv, Cho.) (7)

Read the speech aloud, breathing only at the punctuation points. Support all last words, especially "universe," "sounds," and "watch." Careful—no breath after "dark."

Remember these clues:
- The words ride out on the breath, just send them
- Inhaling gives you a moment to grasp your next line
- Breathe at every opportunity
- If you cut a breathing point, do it intentionally because you don't need it

- Strong breath enables you to speak with power
- Lack of breath signals *weakness.*

What about the common modern habit, especially among film actors, of releasing breath immediately before speaking? This technique is one of many that actors pay good money to learn in various film acting classes. By using it, you lose power and energy, and you probably run out of breath before reaching the end of the spoken line, thus giving you that "fade-away" sound. Whereas some actors and directors believe this approach produces a more "natural" sound, persons who respect language and the actor's gift of voice shun it. You need energy and power to speak well. The idea of allowing the microphone to produce your sound for you kills energy, and that weakens your ability to command the listener—even on film.

So pause awhile ...

Now spend any remaining time reading your material aloud and breathing at the correct places as marked in your text. Apply everything we've discussed.

> *I would applaud thee to the very echo,*
> *That should applaud again.*
> MACBETH, V, iii

Always read and work on Shakespeare aloud. This language is meant to be spoken, and much of the sense is discovered through speech. Shakespeare doesn't just "work better" aloud, it works *ten times better!* Therefore, when you work on the lines, use the opportunity to practice breathing and voice skills as well.

CHARACTER

I lied. We never got to "character." Or did we? If you've applied what we've discussed to your material—scansion, phrasing and discovering antithesis, kicking the box, and correct breathing—a character choice has probably emerged all by itself.

If not, develop one. Now you know what the language is doing and what it requires. Apply everything you already know about creating honest and truthful character, and create! Develop the kind of character that would do and say what the language is doing and saying. The character is that person who needs and uses these words. Do your language study before rehearsals begin, then the rehearsal process can be about character and relationships, as it should be.

To explore in more detail how the character you've selected uses your analysis of the language to come alive through the language, here is one more example. Juliet waits impatiently for the Nurse to bring word of Romeo. Her image-rich lines start like this:

Juliet: Gallop apace, you fiery-footed steeds,
           Towards Phoebus' lodging! Such a wagoner
           As Phaeton would whip you to the west
           And bring in cloudy night immediately.   (*Rom*, III, ii)

As the actor playing Juliet, your text analysis of these four lines will tell you many things about the character, including:
- She thinks in images
- She thinks in classical images ("fiery-footed steeds," "Phoebus' lodging," "wagoner as Phaeton")
- She's had a solid education to know these classical images (she understands that Phoebus is the sun god and his "lodging" is beyond the western horizon, which, when entered, causes night; and Phaeton is his son, with whom the horses of the sun ran away and set fire to the earth, just as the Nurse is bringing "fire" to her)
- She's no "softy" ("whip you")
- She's impatient ("gallop apace," "whip you," "bring . . . immediately.")
- Something is happening too slowly for her (the Nurse is too slow returning)
- She's longing for the night ("bring in cloudy night"), and it's still day ("to the west")
- She thinks of gods controlling her destiny (gods pull the sun across the sky and control day and night—and everything else as well)
- She allows herself to be impatient with these gods, not just with the Nurse

You can probably find more, but that's the idea of what has come from your text analysis.

The character is the person who needs and uses these words. Juliet's education must be deeply imbedded in her mind, because it is clearly released as her passion for Romeo explodes. Your Juliet will choose what she thinks of Phaeton and the speed with which he runs his out-of-control chariot of the sun, and that choice will be clear in the way you read the words. You can make the choice, because you know exactly what the words mean. Your Juliet will choose how rapidly she wants night to descend, and that choice will be clear in the way you read those words.

As the actor, you know what the words are doing—they are allowing the character to expose her emotional state through her learning—so you choose your way of doing it. The way you play Juliet is your choice. But it is based on knowing exactly what Juliet is saying, not guessing what she is saying, and not trusting to "natural talent" to read Shakespeare's lines.

Your Juliet might elect to make more or less of "immediately." Obviously she could be extremely lustful (one reading), or simply eager (another reading). These are the choices you make that make the character your own. But the author is being served now, and the audience will have every opportunity to hear your choices clearly. You know what you're saying, so the audience will know what you're saying.

We probably all agree that understanding the language will not, by itself, make you a good Shakespearean actor. Moving the words from your brain to the audience's ears still requires all the skill and talent you possess, your trained voice (not a "fall-away" sound), plus your huge energy, and every glimmer of passion that is appropriate for each moment.

The task of acting the play through the character is still up to you, the actor. But when acting Shakespeare, if you complete text study before you begin characterization, you stand the best chance of success.

It takes vivid imagination and great technique to be an actor, plus courage, talent, and drive. Add to your imaginative qualities the skills you just relearned, and be successful with Shakespeare!

> *And smooth success*
> *Be strewed before your feet!*
> ANTONY AND CLEOPATRA, I, iii

END OF THE PROFESSIONAL ACTOR'S ONE-DAY BRUSH UP

Break a leg!

> *Well, breathe awhile, then to it again.*
> HENRY IV, PART I, II, iv

> *Tomorrow to the field.*
> ALL'S WELL THAT ENDS WELL, III, i

Resources

We may live to have need of such a verse.

TROILUS AND CRESSIDA, IV, iv

CHAPTER 17

More Exercises

Together with the exercises included in the main text (e.g., kick the box), here are a few others. Each addresses a specific problem. When practicing them, many new discoveries will be made.

I have used these exercises for more than twenty years and can no longer remember where they originated. They are probably combinations of exercises from Stanislavski, Meisner, Berry, Barton, Linklater, Rodenburg, various student and professional actors, and me, and have been sifted, changed, and reinvented while I coached actors and read anything written on the subject of acting, speaking, or analyzing Shakespeare. So acknowledgment is given here to all coaches, directors, teachers, actors, and authors whose influence has helped me to develop these exercises and to pass them along to others without taking personal credit for more than a small share of their effectiveness.

REMEDIES FOR COMMON ACTOR AILMENTS

What to do if:
- *The actor is emphasizing the wrong words.*
  Exercise: Tap out the stresses (chapters 4, 11, and 14).
- *The actor is not phrasing correctly.*
  Exercise: Phrasing exercise (chapters 3, 11, and 15).
- *The actor is not supporting the line through to the end.*
  Exercise: Kick the box (chapters 4, 11, and 16).
- *The actor is not breathing correctly.*
  Exercise: Breathing exercises (chapters 5, 11, and 16).
- *The tempo and rhythm are off, because the actor is playing unnecessary subtext.*

Exercise: Removing subtext (chapters 6 and 15).
- *The actor is not emphasizing the antithetical words, thoughts, and phrases.*
Exercise: Playing the antithesis (chapters 8 and 15).
- *The actor is not properly opening his/her mouth.*
Running and shouting the lines will open the mouth and release the words with energy. Also, singing the lines like an Italian tenor or dramatic soprano to any made-up tune opens the voice and also calls attention to each syllable, because when singing, each syllable gets its own note.
- *The actor is not listening.*
The partner should suddenly whisper the lines. Whispering demands attention. Also, speak the scene in total darkness.
- *The actor is not using the vowel sounds.*
Read the lines speaking *only* the vowels. The actor will discover the wonderful vowel sounds and the opportunities they offer.
- *The actor is rushing, or is locked into rote memorization.*
  1. The actor who is rushing should read the lines for the listening actor to mime. The actor must slow down and clarify each thought, or the mime can't perform.
  2. Use the phrasing exercise from the text, moving on punctuation points.
  3. Perform a physical or mental task while speaking the lines. For example, draw a picture of a specific object on the chalkboard while speaking the lines, or multiply a complex number on the chalkboard while speaking the lines, or arrange the other actors according to last names or height while speaking the lines. When speaking while concentrating on a different task, the actor will find new emphasis for specific words and will automatically slow down.
  4. Two actors sit back-to-back on the floor after having memorized fifteen to twenty lines of a scene. The actor with the opening line says first in her own words what she is going to say via Shakespeare's lines, then speaks the lines. The second actor repeats in his own words what he heard, then states in his own words what he is going to say via Shakespeare's lines, then speaks the lines. This continues until the actors have worked through the scene. Then speak the scene again, but only with Shakespeare's words.

     You can create variations on this exercise, all of which will help actors listen, phrase, discover new ideas, and find tempo. This is an excellent exercise.
- *The actor's voice is high pitched.*
  1. Sit on the floor holding your knees, and rock gently and speak. Feel your voice lower itself in your body. Try to retain that voice when you stand up.
  2. Lie on the floor on your back, and begin speaking your lines. Your voice will slowly lower in pitch. When it is low and strong and supported, stand up without losing that voice. Memorize its placement.
- *The actor has no passion.*
The actor doesn't understand what the character is actually doing. Use analysis to solve that problem first. Then, you might try this technical exercise: Create a resistance. For example, have the actor to whom the first actor is speaking refuse to stand still or to look at the first actor, yet insist that the first actor make eye contact. The irritation that develops will help free the emotions.

You can create variations on this exercise. The idea is to make it difficult for the speaker to communicate.

- *The actors are over-acting.*
  Try placing a "microphone" (a prop will work) within inches of two actors standing very close together and have them read the scene for "television." When they pull back to video/film acting, they begin to listen and discover and stop "performing."

You will find hundreds of other exercises in the various books listed in the bibliography.

CHAPTER 18

Bibliography

Following are selected lists of (1) successful and unsuccessful examples of acting Shakespeare on film and video, (2) books for further study, (3) books on acting Shakespeare, and (4) books on acting realism.

IA. SELECTED VIDEO AND FILM PERFORMANCES

Hamlet

1996—Kenneth Branagh's film of the uncut text. Superb cast and production values, with wonderful performances in the leading roles. Great clarity of plot and character, without loss of language. Verse handled especially well by Branagh (Hamlet), Derek Jacobi (Claudius), Julie Christie (Gertrude), and Nicholas Farrell (Horatio). Marred only by a few whispering scenes and occasional loud background effects that bury the words. Exchanges between Branagh and Jacobi are especially fine to study.

1990—Franco Zeffirelli's film, starring Mel Gibson (Hamlet), who is attractive and usually comfortable with the language (much of which has been cut) and the role. The strong supporting cast of Glenn Close (Gertrude), Alan Bates (Claudius), Paul Scofield (Ghost), Helena Bonham Carter (Ophelia), Ian Holm (Polonius), and Stephen Dillane (Horatio) handle the verse beautifully. Listen especially to Scofield's Ghost speeches.

1990—New York Shakespeare Festival production produced for video by Kimberly Myers, directed by Kevin Kline with Kirk Browning; with Kline (Hamlet), Peter Francis James (Horatio), Robert Murch (Ghost), Brian Murray (King), Dana Ivey (Queen), Michael Cumpsty (Laertes), Josef Sommer (Polonius), Diane Verona (Ophelia), and

Clement Fowler (Player King). The modern dress and very drab production plays like a melodrama, with considerable "over-the-top" acting. The design and acting style may have worked better in the original stage production, but did not translate well to video. Kline's Hamlet is very watery-eyed and often ineffective. Exceptions include the Hamlet/Ophelia confrontation scene, which has a wonderful interpretation, and Hamlet's relaxed, and yet commanding advice to the players.

1948—Laurence Olivier's black-and-white film, starring Olivier (Hamlet), Jean Simmons (Ophelia), Eileen Herlie (Gertrude), Basil Syndey (Claudius), Felix Aylmer (Polonius), Norman Wooland (Horatio), and Stanley Hollaway (First Gravedigger). Effective performance in many ways, and a solid reading of the text. The technique of soliloquies as voice-overs mixed with live dialogue doesn't quite work, and some scenes are melodramatic. Watch especially Aylmer and Hollaway, who offer classic interpretations of their characters.

Henry V

1989—Kenneth Branagh's film, starring Branagh as the King. Superb cast and production. For the American ear, some articulation problems in the first scene (unintelligible whispering) and with Ian Holm's accent for the Welshman, Fluellen. Paul Scofield is brilliant as the French king, as are Emma Thompson as his daughter, Brian Blessed as Exeter, and Derek Jacobi as Chorus. Branagh's St. Crispan's speech is perfection, as is Blessed's charge to the French king.

1944—Laurence Olivier's film, starring Olivier as the King. The acting style may seem a little rhetorical today, but the film still contains some brilliant work. The opening scene is especially useful to students, as it is Olivier's version of what it was like backstage at the Globe during Shakespeare's day.

Romeo and Juliet

1996—Baz Luhrmann's high energy film, set in modern Los Angeles, with Leonardo DiCaprio (Romeo), Claire Danes (Juliet), Dash Mihok (Benvolio), John Leguizamo (Tybalt), Paul Sorvino (Capulet), Brian Dennehy (Montague), and Harold Perrineau, Jr. (Mercutio). An original adaptation that works as the action film it is intended to be. Effects, however, and a restless camera dominate what little language is retained. The older actors do well, but many of the attractive young actors needed much more vocal work and didn't get it. Some excellent examples of reading lines with full stops, a technique (or lack of) that kills the rhythm and the thought within the verse.

1968—Franco Zeffirelli's wonderful film is almost a classic today. Excellent adaptation of a play to film—with very little dialogue left. Fine language coaching of the young actors, Olivia Hussey and Leonard Whiting. Beautiful visual production.

Richard III

1996—Al Pacino's film, *Looking for Richard*, presents scenes from the play, together with improvisation. With Pacino (Richard), Alec Baldwin (Clarence), Kevin Conway (Hastings), Harris Yulin (Edward IV), Penelope Allen (Queen Elizabeth), Kevin Spacey (Buckingham), Winona Ryder (Lady Anne), Estelle Parsons (Queen Margaret), Aidan Quinn (Richmond), and includes comments on Shakespeare from Kevin

Kline, Kenneth Branagh, James Earl Jones, Rosemary Harris, Peter Brook, Derek Jacobi, John Gielgud, and Vanessa Redgrave. A successful documentary film containing both comments and acted scenes. Pacino's untrained voice creates a breathy acting style that seems indulgent. This and Baldwin's subtextual style are the direct opposites of Conway and Allen, plus some of the others, who play the heightened text extremely well. Good opportunity to compare acting styles.

1995—Richard Loncraine's film, starring Ian McKellen (Richard), Annette Bening (Elizabeth), Nigel Hawthorne (Clarence), Robert Downey, Jr. (Rivers), Jim Broadbent (Buckingham), Maggie Smith (Duchess of York), John Wood (King Edward), and Kristin Scholl Thomas (Lady Anne). This original and compelling adaptation sets the story in the fascist 1930s. The locale mostly works, and the characters are real. McKellen is outstanding in the title role, having adjusted his performance from the original stage production to film without a hitch. Superb example of character and language in harmony.

1955—Laurence Olivier's film, starring Olivier (Richard), Ralph Richardson (Buckingham), Claire Bloom (Lady Anne), and John Gielgud (Clarence). Olivier changed the soliloquy technique used in his earlier *Hamlet* and now speaks directly into the camera, with marvelous effect and brilliant characterization. A superb accomplishment. Watch especially the soliloquies, and note the superior example of how to hold a thought for forty-one lines in a Shakespearean speech. Olivier does this in his opening soliloquy.

Othello

1996—Oliver Parker's film, starring Laurence Fishburne (Othello), Kenneth Branagh (Iago), and Irene Jacob (Desdemona). Some wonderful acting and directing, but marred by an overdose of breathy whispering, which makes various scenes unintelligible and irritating.

1965—BHE Production from the National Theatre of Great Britain. Stuart Burge's film starring Laurence Olivier (Othello), Frank Finlay (Iago), Maggie Smith (Desdemona), Joyce Redman (Emelia), and Derek Jacobi (Cassio). Originally directed for the stage by John Dexter. Excellent example of an actor (Olivier) developing a voice for a character, and the language is handled beautifully. Smith creates a "mature," but effective Desdemona. Jacobi and Finlay are both excellent.

Macbeth

1978—Thames Television Video Stage taping of Trevor Nunn's 1976 Royal Shakespeare Company production, produced by Nunn, starring Ian McKellen (Macbeth), Judi Dench (Lady Macbeth), John Woodvine (Banquo), Griffith James (Duncan), Roger Rees (Malcolm), and Bob Peck (Macduff). With a "black-and-white" design scheme, the play is presented by only sixteen actors and limited props and sets. Each scene is played against a black background. The camera is always tight, and soliloquies are into the lens. The production values, which probably worked better on stage, become dull on tape—more like a formal reading than a stage production. But the language is handled beautifully.

1976—Roman Polanski's film, starring Jon Finch (Macbeth) and Francesca Annis (Lady Macbeth). An excellent film, with fine acting and beautiful production values. Only the voice-over soliloquies become tiresome.

1948—Orson Welles' eighty-nine–minute film adaptation, with effective black-and-white photography. The soliloquies, all voice-overs, are melodramatic, but Welles is commanding as Macbeth, and Jeanette Nolan's Lady Macbeth is engaging, despite an acting style more suited to the stage. The film was low budget and shot in twenty-three days.

1957—Akira Kurosawa's adaptation of the story for his film, entitled *Throne of Blood*, follows the plot with "Lady Macbeth" given new motivations. Toshiro Mifune and Isuzu Yamada star. Beautiful black-and-white photography. In Japanese with sub-titles.

King Lear

1997—BBC/WGBN video of a Royal National Theatre production, directed by Richard Eyre, with Ian Holm (Lear), Michael Bryant (Fool), David Burke (Kent), Barbara Flynn (Goneril), Amanda Redman (Regan), Victoria Hamilton (Cordelia), and Timothy West (Gloucester). Clear and easy-to-follow production, with Holm strong as Lear. The cast is wonderful, and the language is read beautifully.

1984—Michael Elliott's film, starring Laurence Olivier (Lear), Colin Blakely (Kent), Anna Calder-Marshall (Cordelia), Dorothy Tutin (Goneril), Diana Rigg (Regan), and John Hurt (Fool). Wonderful film, with excellent scenes for study, especially between Lear/Fool and Lear/Kent. Olivier's frail, real-life condition helps to creates marvelous empathy for Lear (or Lear/Olivier). The actor's last film.

1971—Grigori Kozintsev's film, with screenplay by Boris Pasternak. Beautifully filmed in black-and-white. Wonderful costume, prop, and setting design, probably the twelfth or thirteenth century (soldiers have cannon, but no muskets), with a revealing look at Lear's retinue, an entourage that would discourage any potential host. Starring Yuri Jarvet (Lear), E. Radzins (Goneril), G. Volcher (Regan), V. Shendrikova (Cordelia), O. Dal (Fool), K. Sebris (Glouster) [sic], and E. Melyandov (Kent). Production has many nice touches, like Cordelia's wedding scene, and follows the original story quite closely. Translated from verse to Russian, then translated back for the subtitles, the language now reads like heightened prose, with very few of the original lines intact.

1970—Royal Shakespeare Company film, directed by Peter Brook, in black-and-white photography, starring Paul Scofield (Lear) and Irene Worth (Goneril). Example of a "heavy" approach to Shakespeare—slow and ponderous; yet some wonderful scenes and characterizations, if you are willing to wait. This production certainly worked better on stage, but did not translate well to film.

1985—Japanese director Akira Kurosawa's film is roughly based on Shakespeare's story of King Lear. Entitled *Ran*, Japanese for "chaos." Magnificent visual and spoken production. In Japanese with English subtitles.

Julius Caesar
1970—Stuart Burge's film, starring John Gielgud (Caesar), Charlton Heston (Antony), Jason Robards (Brutus), and Richard Johnson (Cassius). Gielgud's strong performance of Caesar is overthrown by a few weak ones, notably Robards' subtextual acting style, which kills the verse. Among the Americans, Heston and Robert Vaughn (Casca) fare better.

1953—John Houseman's and Joseph L. Mankiewicz's film, starring Marlon Brando (Antony), James Mason (Brutus), John Gielgud (Cassius), and Louis Calhern (Caesar). Gielgud's Cassius and Mason's Brutus are classics. Brando learned to handle the verse and does not rely entirely on subtext, thus offering an effective performance. However, the acting styles are an exercise in contrast. Worth studying for this interesting variety.

The Taming of the Shrew
1986—Stratford Shakespeare Festival (Canada) video of a live performance, directed by Peter Dews, starring Len Cariou (Petruchio). Superb production, probably the best of this play on tape or film. Cariou's and Sharry Flett's (Kate) wooing scene the best ever. Magnificent handling of the language and marvelous characters throughout. Worth studying everything Cariou does.

1975—Video of an American Conservatory Theatre production, directed by William Ball and starring Marc Singer (Petruchio), Fredi Olster (Kate), and William Paterson (Baptista). Ball elects to shape the play as *Commedia dell'arte*, and the actors are marvelous at playing the *lazzi* in this very lovely production. However, the style begins to dominate the language and the play itself, and one looks forward to the "quiet" moments. The "wooing scene" and Kate's final scene are especially fine, because the actors abandon the "style" and play the language and situation, sans effects. Excellent example of applying a preconceived physicalization to heightened text with mixed results.

1966—Franco Zeffirelli's film, starring Richard Burton and Elizabeth Taylor. Beautiful visual production. Burton strong, if a little old for the role. Excellent example of an American actress, Taylor, in a gutsy effort, successful in many ways, while working with limited vocal power.

A Midsummer Night's Dream
1999—Michael Hoffman's film (director and screenplay), with a cast of American, British, and French actors, including Kevin Kline (Bottom), Rupert Everett (Oberon), Michelle Pfeiffer (Titania), Stanley Tucci (Puck), Calista Flockhart (Helena), Anna Friel (Hermia), Christian Bale (Demetrious), Dominic West (Lysander), Roger Rees (Peter Quince), David Strathairn (Theseus), and Sophie Marceau (Hippolyta). A visually beautiful film (Gabriella Pescucci, costume design, and Luciana Arrighi, production design), with a gorgeous musical score, selected mostly from Italian operas. A serious effort to capture the play on film. Yet the film bogs down in indulgent acting, especially from Pfeiffer and Everett, and uncertainty how to handle the lovers, who are beautiful and capable with the language, but just get boring. Kline, cast against type, takes getting used to as Bottom. But together with Tucci and Rees, he handles

Shakespeare's language as it should be spoken, and his dream speech is the highlight of the film. The final-act play offered by the mechanicals almost salvages the film. Worth viewing for both strengths and weaknesses.

1996—RSC video of an Adrian Noble production, with Stella Gonet (Hippolyta/ Titania), Alex Jennings (Theseus/Oberon), Desmond Barrit (Bottom), Barry Lynch (Puck/Philostrate), Monica Doan (Hermia), and Hayden Gwyne (Helena). Workers and fairies also doubled in this colorful modern-dress production. The mechanicals are especially fine, and all the language is beautifully read.

1969—Royal Shakespeare Company film, directed by Peter Hall, with Diana Rigg (Helena), Helen Mirren (Hermia), David Warner (Lysander), Michael Jayston (Demetrius), Ian Richardson (Oberon), Judi Dench (Titania), and Ian Holm (Puck). Excellent examples of language handled to near perfection, while offering honest characters. Clear script without too much cutting.

Twelfth Night
1998—Video of a "Live from Lincoln Center" production, directed by Nicholas Hytner, starring Helen Hunt (Viola), Philip Bosco (Malvolio), Kyra Sedgwick (Olivia), Brian Murray (Sir Toby), Max Wright (Sir Andrew), Paul Rudd (Orsino), and Amy Hill (Maria). Wonderful production, with excellent examples of American actors handling Shakespeare's verse with confidence, a credit to the director's superb sense of language.

1996—BBC film, adapted and directed by Trevor Nunn, starring Ben Kingsley (Feste), Imogen Stubbs (Viola), Helena Bohnam Carter (Olivia), Nigel Hawthorne (Malvolio), Toby Stephens (Orsino), Mel Smith (Sir Toby), and Richard E. Grant (Sir Andrew). Excellent film in all ways. Some fascinating scenes of simultaneous action. Superb cast. Marred only by heavy whispering in places, which kills the dialogue. Probably as good a production of the play on film as will be seen in a long time.

Much Ado About Nothing
1993—Kenneth Branagh's film, starring Branagh (Benedick) and Emma Thompson (Beatrice). Wonderful film, especially the scenes between the two outstanding leads. Marred only by a few American film actors who attempt to force character on the language and struggle with the verse. Worth studying for both examples.

1973—Video of a New York Shakespeare Festival and CBS Television production, brilliantly directed by A. J. Antoon with Nick Havinga. Wonderful and colorful 1900 American design by Tom John and Theoni V. Aldredge, with a sparkling musical score by Peter Link. The American actors handle the language extremely well, led by Kathleen Widdoes (Beatrice), Sam Waterston (Benedick), Glenn Walken (Claudio), April Shawhan (Hero), Douglas Watson (Don Pedro), and Barnard Hughes (Dogberry). May be viewed at the New York Public Library for the Performing Arts.

As You Like It
1986—Stratford Shakespeare Festival (Canada) video of a live performance, directed by John Hirsch. Wonderful taping of a stage production, with a strong cast and first-

class production values. The verse is spoken beautifully by Roberta Maxwell (Rosalind), Andrew Gillies (Orlando), Rosemary Dunsmore (Celia), Nicholas Pennell (Jaques), Lewis Gordon (Touchstone), and most of the others.

All's Well That Ends Well
1978—Video of a New York Shakespeare Festival production, skillfully directed by Wilford Leach with fabulous music by Richard Weinstock. Beautiful production designed by Wilford Leach (sets), Jennifer Tipton (lights), and Carol Oditz (costumes), starring Pamela Reed (Helena), Mark Linn Baker (Bertram), Elizabeth Wilson (Countess), Remak Ramsay (King of France), Frances Conroy (Diana), John Ferraro (Levatch), and Larry Pine (Parolles). Excellent direction that brings out all the humor—the actors occasionally break into song. First class in every way, with American actors correctly handling the verse. May be viewed at the New York Public Library for the Performing Arts.

The Merchant of Venice
1973—John Sichel's video of Jonathan Miller's 1970 National Theatre Company stage production, starring Laurence Olivier (Shylock), Joan Plowright (Portia), Jeremy Brett (Bassanio), and Michael Jayston (Gratiano). The video recaptures the stage production and adds a few more settings. Excellent handling of the verse and wonderful examples of playing subtext without indulging in character or sacrificing the rhythm of the language. Very bold acting, which may seem "large" for film.

IB. OTHER FILMS AND VIDEOS

1984—*Playing Shakespeare.* The Royal Shakespeare Company series of video workshops on the techniques and problems of acting Shakespeare. Host John Barton is accompanied by a dozen actors from the RSC. Excellent examples. A must for all acting programs. Barton's text of the same title is a transcription of the workshops.

1999—*The Working Shakespeare Video Library.* Applause Books' workshop series, produced by Glenn Young, hosted by Jeremy Irons, and taught by Cicely Berry and Andrew Wade. A six-video series similar to John Barton's *Playing Shakespeare*, but more current and featuring a combination of American and British actors, including Claire Danes, Blythe Danner, Lindsay Duncan, Samuel L. Jackson, Victor Garber, Helen Hunt, Robert Sean Leonard, Toby Stephens, Diane Venora, and Emily Watson. Wonderful demonstrations of the techniques of handling Shakespeare's language.

1999—*Shakespeare in Love.* Miramax Film, directed by John Madden, written by Tom Stoppard and Mark Norman, with Joseph Fiennes, Gwyneth Paltrow, Colin Firth, Geoffrey Rush, Ben Affleck, Judi Dench, and Rupert Everett. Exquisite film, set in sixteenth century England. Madden and his writers create a fictional, and comic, background for the young Shakespeare to create *Romeo and Juliet*. Verse from the play and the non-stage language are handled beautifully by this company of mostly RSC actors. First class in every way.

1982—*Acting Shakespeare: Ian McKellen on Broadway.* CBS Broadcast Center Video of McKellen's one-man show, taped live. Stage production directed by Sean Mathias, produced by Andrew Susskind, directed for television by Kirk Browning. McKellen talks about Shakespeare and performs a dozen or so monologues quite successfully. One of the world's best Shakespearean actors, McKellen is especially good at blending language with character. For actors new to Shakespeare, he offers an informative section on character (Macbeth) and verse analysis, then performs it.

1991—*Prospero's Books.* A Miramax Film. Peter Greenaway's version of *The Tempest,* with John Gielgud speaking most of the dialogue for all characters. Beautifully designed production, with engaging special effects. However, unless you are very familiar with the source, much of this story will be confusing. The narrative approach, with visuals inserted, becomes tedious and creates a split focus. Quite erotic.

1966—*Chimes at Midnight (Falstaff).* An International and Société des Films Sirius, Harry Saltzman film, conceived and directed by Orson Welles, with Welles (Falstaff), John Gielgud, Norman Rodway, Margaret Rutherford, Jeanne Moreau, and Keith Baxter, narrated by Ralph Richardson. A lovely collection of the Falstaff scenes from (mostly) *Henry IV* (both parts), with Welles a remarkable Sir John. Beautifully acted, wonderful scenes to study.

1992—*Shakespeare: the Animated Tales.* Random House Home Video adapted six of the plays to thirty-minute animation treatment for the child audience. Primarily animated characters with narration. Tapes are available for *Hamlet, Macbeth, A Midsummer Night's Dream, Romeo and Juliet, The Tempest,* and *Twelfth Night.*

Productions of all of Shakespeare's plays were taped for the BBC Shakespeare Series between 1979 and 1984 and are available in most libraries. Quality is mixed, but overall, the series is a remarkable achievement, valued by everyone who enjoys the plays.

In 1989, shortly before the end of its theatrical existence, the English Shakespeare Company, with Michael Pennington as artistic director, taped live performances of seven of the history plays in a series called *The Wars of the Roses.* The plays were produced in modern or "eclectic" dress. Sound quality is a problem. The videos are available online from Facets Video at *www.facets.org.*

About 350 films or videos of Shakespeare's plays are currently available, dating back to Herbert Beerbohm Tree's direction of an 1899 silent film version of *King John,* in which Beerbohm Tree also starred. With interest high in feature films of Shakespeare's plays, and with many stage companies now videotaping productions, this number, which was reached after one hundred years, will double in the next ten. For current information on films and videos, refer to the Shakespeare Filmography online at *http://us.imdb.com/name?Shakespeare,+william.*

For fast ordering or tracking of a Shakespearean video or CD, a small store in Stratford, Ontario, Canada, is unusually well-stocked and willing to help you find a video or CD if they don't have it. Contact the Poor Yorick CD and Video Emporium, Tanya Gough, Proprietrix, by e-mail at *yorick@bardcentral.net,* or see their complete catalogue and prices online at *www.bardcentral.com,* or call (519) 272-1999. The complete address is: Poor Yorick CD & Video Emporium, 89a Downie Street, Stratford, Ontario, Canada, N5A 1W8.

2. BOOKS FOR FURTHER STUDY

This list includes all works consulted for this book, some of which are mentioned in the text, and some other books useful to the actor.

Bartlett, John, ed. *A Complete Concordance to Shakespeare*. 18th ed. New York: St. Martin's, 1984.

Barton, John. *Playing Shakespeare*. London: Methuen, 1984.

Berry, Cicely. *The Actor and the Text*. New York: Scribner's, 1988.

Berry, Ralph. *The Shakespearean Metaphor: Studies in Language and Form*. Totowa, N.J.: Rawmon and Littlefield, 1978.

Bevington, David, ed. *The Complete Works of Shakespeare*. 4th ed. New York: HarperCollins, 1992.

Bloom, Harold. *Shakespeare: The Invention of the Human*. New York: Riverhead Books, 1998.

Boorstin, Daniel J. *The Americans: The National Experience*. New York: Random House, 1965.

Booth, Stephen. *Shakespeare's Sonnets*. New Haven: Yale University Press, 1977.

Bosco, Philip. Philip Bosco speaks out. *In Theatre*. 7 August 1998, 23–25.

Brook, Peter. *The Empty Space*. New York: Atheneum, 1968.

―――. *Evoking Shakespeare*. New York: Theatre Communications Group, 1998.

Brown, John Russell. *Discovering Shakespeare*. New York: Columbia University Press, 1981.

―――. *Free Shakespeare*. London: Heinemann, 1974.

―――. *Shakespeare's Dramatic Style*. London: Heinemann, 1970.

―――. *Shakespeare's Plays in Performance*. Revised Edition. New York: Applause, 1993.

―――. *William Shakespeare: Writing for Performance*. New York: St. Martin's Press, 1996.

Bulman, James C. *Shakespeare, Theory, and Performance*. London and New York: Routledge, 1966.

Burson, Linda. *Play with Shakespeare*. Charlottesville, Va.: New Plays Books, 1992.

Cercignani, Fausto. *Shakespeare's Words and Elizabethan Pronunciation*. Oxford: Oxford University Press, 1981.

Davis, James E. and Ronald Salomone, eds. *Teaching Shakespeare Today*. Urbana, Il.: National Council of Teachers of English, 1993.

―――. *Teaching Shakespeare into the Twenty-First Century*. Urbana, Il.: National Council of Teachers of English, 1997.

Doyle, John and Roy Lischner. *Shakespeare for Dummies*. Foster City, CA: IDG Books, 1999.

Epstein, Morrie. *The Friendly Shakespeare*. New York: Viking Penguin, 1993.

Freeman, Neil, ed. *Applause First Folio Editions*. New York: Applause, 1998 and on. (Shakespeare's thirty-six plays in modern print, available individually).

―――. *The Applause First Folio of Shakespeare: in Modern Type*. New York: Applause, 2000.

―――. *Folio Scripts: Shakespeare's First Texts*. 2nd ed. Vancouver: Self-published, distributed by Applause Books, 1999.

Gielgud, John. *Backward Glances*. London: Hodder & Stoughton, 1989.

―――. and John Miller. *Acting Shakespeare*. New York: Scribner's, 1991.

Granville-Barker, Harley. *Prefaces to Shakespeare*. 4 vols. Princeton: Princeton University Press, 1946.

———— and G. B. Harrison. *A Companion to Shakespeare Studies*. New York: Doubleday, 1960.

Guthrie, Tyrone. *A Life in the Theatre*. New York: McGraw-Hill, 1959.

————. *In Various Directions: A View of the Theatre*. New York: Macmillan, 1965.

Halio, Jay L. *Understanding Shakespeare's Plays in Performance*. Manchester: Manchester University Press, 1988.

Hall, Peter. *Peter Hall's Diaries*. Ed. John Goodwin. London: Hamish Hamilton, 1983.

Harbage, Alfred, ed. *William Shakespeare: The Complete Works*. Revised Edition. *The Complete Pelican Shakespeare*. New York: Viking Penguin, 1977.

Hinman, Charlton, ed. *The First Folio of Shakespeare: The Norton Facsimile*. New York: W.W. Norton, 1968.

Joseph, Miriam. *Shakespeare's Use of the Arts of Language*. New York: Hafner, 1947.

Kerrigan, John, ed. *William Shakespeare: The Sonnets and A Lover's Complaint*. New York: Viking Penguin, 1986.

Mahood, M. M. *Playing Bit Parts in Shakespeare*. New York: Routledge, 1998.

Mamet, David. *True and False: Heresy and Common Sense for the Actor*. New York: Pantheon, 1997.

Martin, Jacqueline. *Voice in Modern Theatre*. New York: Routledge, 1991.

McCrum, Robert, William Cran, and Robert MacNeil. *The Story of English*. New York: Viking, 1986.

Michaels, Wendy. *Playbuilding Shakespeare*. Cambridge: Cambridge University Press, 1996

Miller, Arthur. *A View From the Bridge*. In *Drama: An Introductory Anthology*, Otto Reinert ed. Boston: Little, Brown, 1961.

Moore, Sonia. *The Stanislavsky System*. Revised Edition. New York: Viking, 1965.

O'Brian, Peggy, ed. *Shakespeare Set Free*. Series of three books. New York: Washington Square Press, 1993.

Olivier, Laurence. *On Acting*. New York: Simon and Schuster, 1986.

Onions, C. T. A. *Shakespeare Glossary*. 3rd ed. Revised. Robert D. Eagleson. Oxford: Clarendon Press, 1986.

Parsons, Keith and Pamela Mason, eds. *Shakespeare in Performance*. London: Salamander Books, 1995.

Proudfit, Scott. Genius in exile. *Back Stage West*, 10 June 1999, 6.

Reynolds, Peter. *Teaching Shakespeare*. Oxford: Oxford University Press, 1997.

Robinson, Randal. *Unlocking Shakespeare's Language*. Urbana, Il.: National Council of Teachers of English, 1988.

Rowse, A. L. *The England of Elizabeth*. New York: Macmillan, 1950.

Rozett, Martha Tuck. *Talking Back to Shakespeare*. Urbana, Il.: National Council of Teachers of English, 1994.

Rygiel, Mary Ann. *Shakespeare Among School Children*. Urbana, Il.: National Council of Teachers of English, 1992.

Schmidt, Alexander. *The Shakespeare Lexicon: A Complete Dictionary of the English Words, Phrases and Construction in the Works of the Poet*. 3rd ed. Revised by Gregor Sarrazin. 2 vols. Berlin: G. Reimer, 1902.

Shakespeare, William. "Writer Filmography." Online. Available from Internet Movie Database, 1999, at *http://us.imdb.com/name?Shakespeare,+william*.

Shaw, George Bernard. *Man and Superman*. In *Seven Plays by Bernard Shaw*. New

York: Dodd, Mead & Company, 1951.

Spain, Delbert. *Shakespeare Sounded Soundly: The Verse Structure and the Language.* Santa Barbara, CA: Capra, 1988.

Spurgeon, Caroline F. E. *Shakespeare's Imagery and What It Tells Us.* Cambridge: Cambridge University Press, 1935.

Tillyard, E. M. W. *The Elizabethan World Picture.* New York: Vintage, 1941.

Toropov, Brandon. *Shakespeare for Beginners.* New York: Writers and Readers, 1997.

Vendler, Helen Hennessy. *The Art of Shakespeare's Sonnets.* Cambridge: Harvard University Press, 1997.

Whitney, Craig R. Hoffman as Shylock: London critics cool. *New York Times,* 3 June 1989, A13.

3. BOOKS ON ACTING SHAKESPEARE

The bibliography of books about the skills required to act Shakespeare is slim. Many of the useful books are actually voice studies. But each book listed here is helpful to the actor in one way or another.

Barton, John. *Playing Shakespeare.* London: Methuen, 1984.

Berry, Cicely. *The Actor and the Text.* New York: Scribner's, 1988.

———. *Voice and the Actor.* New York: Macmillan, 1973.

Berry, Ralph. *On Directing Shakespeare: Interviews with Contemporary Directors.* London: Hamish Hamilton, 1989.

Bevington, David. *Acting is Eloquence: Shakespeare's Language of Gesture.* Cambridge: Harvard University Press, 1984.

Brine, Adrian and Michael York. *A Shakespearean Actor Prepares.* North Stratford, NH: Smith and Kraus, 1999.

Brockbank, Philip, ed. *Players of Shakespeare: Essays in Shakespearean Performance by Twelve Players with the Royal Shakespeare Company.* Cambridge: Cambridge University Press, 1985.

Brown, John Russell, ed. *Shakescenes: Shakespeare for Two.* New York: Applause Books, 1992.

Brubaker, Edward S. *Shakespeare Aloud: A Guide to His Verse on Stage.* Lancaster, Pa.: Author, 1976.

Cohen, Robert. *Acting in Shakespeare.* Mountain View, Ca.: Mayfield, 1991.

Daw, Kurt. *Acting Shakespeare & His Contemporaries.* Portsmouth, N.H.: Heinemann, 1998.

Guthrie, Tyrone. *Tyrone Guthrie on Acting.* New York: Viking, 1971.

Jackson, Russell and Robert Smallwood, eds. *Players of Shakespeare 2: Further Essays in Shakespearean Performance by Players with the Royal Shakespeare Company.* Cambridge: Cambridge University Press, 1988.

Joseph, Bertram. *Acting Shakespeare.* Revised Edition. New York: Theatre Arts Books, 1969.

———. *A Shakespeare Workbook.* 2 vols. New York: Theatre Arts Books, 1980.

Linklater, Kristin. *Freeing Shakespeare's Voice.* New York: Theatre Communications Group, 1992.

Rodenburg, Patsy. *The Actor Speaks: Voice and the Performer.* London: Methuen, 1998.

———. *The Need for Words.* New York: Routledge, 1993.

———. *The Right to Speak*. New York: Routledge, 1992.

Sher, Antony. *Year of the King*. New York: Limelight Editions, 1986.

Spain, Delbert. *Shakespeare Sounded Soundly: The Verse Structure and the Language*. Santa Barbara, Ca.: Capra Press, 1988.

Suzman, Janet. *Acting with Shakespeare: Three Comedies*. New York: Applause Books, 1996.

Woods, Leigh. *On Playing Shakespeare: Advice and Commentary from Actors and Actresses of the Past*. New York: Greenwood, 1991.

4. BOOKS ON ACTING REALISM

Most of the classic books on acting, and the better new ones, are not concerned with playing verse. Shakespeare is rarely mentioned. Yet, these are excellent books that deal with acting primarily as it relates to modern text for stage or film.

Adler, Stella. *The Technique of Acting*. New York: Bantam, 1988.

Boleslavsky, Richard. *Acting: The First Six Lessons*. New York: Theatre Arts Books, 1933.

Chekhov, Michael. *On the Technique of Acting*. New York: HarperCollins, 1991; reprint and revised, *To the Actor*. New York: Barnes and Noble, 1985.

Bruder, Melissa, et al. *A Practical Handbook for the Actor*. New York: Vintage, 1986.

Hagen, Uta. *A Challenge for the Actor*. New York: Charles Scribner's Sons, 1991.

——— and Haskel Frankel. *Respect for Acting*. New York: Macmillan, 1973.

Mamet, David. *True or False: Heresy and Common Sense for the Actor*. New York: Pantheon, 1997.

Meisner, Sanford and Dennis Longwell. *Sanford Meisner on Acting*. New York: Random House, 1987.

Moore, Sonya. *The Stanislavski System*. Revised Edition. New York: Viking, 1965.

———. *Training an Actor*. New York: Viking, 1968.

Shapiro, Mel. *An Actor Performs*. Fort Worth, TX: Harcourt Brace, 1997.

Silverberg, Larry. *The Sanford Meisner Approach*. 2 vols. Lynn, NH: Smith and Kraus, 1994 (Vol 1), 1997 (Vol 2). Two more volumes are in preparation.

Stanislavski, Constantine. *An Actor Prepares*. Trans. Elizabeth Reynolds Hapgood. New York: Routledge, 1936.

———. *My Life in Art*. Trans. J. J. Robbins. New York: Theatre Arts Books, 1924, reprint, New York: Little, Brown, 1948.

———. *Building a Character*. Trans. Elizabeth Reynolds Hapgood. New York: Theatre Arts Books, 1949.

Glossary of Terms

These terms are defined as they apply to acting Shakespeare.

Alexandrine—a six-foot verse line, usually with twelve syllables, e.g., "A thousand times more fair, ten thousand times more rich;" (*MV*, III, ii). Also called iambic hexameter.

alliteration—sequential words beginning with the same letter, e.g., Antony's "For I have neither writ, nor words, nor worth," (*JC*, III, ii).

ambiguity—uncertainty of meaning or intention; double meaning in a word or phrase; opposite of being clear or certain. The actor must play both the surface meaning and the second meaning, e.g., after being fatally wounded by Tybalt, Mercutio remarks, "Ask for me to-morrow, and you shall find me a grave man." (*Rom*, III, i), or Lady Macbeth's comment about smearing Duncan's servants with blood: "If he do bleed, I'll gild the faces of the grooms withal" (*Mac*, ii, ii).

anapest—a foot containing three syllables, the first two unstressed, the third stressed. An anapestic foot. "To be THUS / is NOTH /ing; BUT / to be SAFE / ly THUS" (*Mac*, III, i). Common for words like "amputee" or "put it up." See Delbert Spain's *Shakespeare Sounded Soundly* for study.

anomaly—irregularity; a deviation from the common form; lines which depart from the regular blank verse line, such as those with four or six feet per line, rather than five, or a trochaic measure.

antithesis—opposing words or ideas set against each other, for example, "To be, or not to be—" (*Ham*, III, i), or "Give me liberty or give me death."

blank verse—unrhymed verse, especially unrhymed iambic pentameter.

caesura—a sense break in a blank verse line. Nearly every line will take a caesura after the second or third foot. Also used to set up a single word.

dactyl—a foot containing three syllables, the first stressed followed by two unstressed. A dactylic foot. Common with words like "memory" or "frequently."

elision—omitting a vowel, which results in a shortened word or words, for example, int'rest for interest, degen'rate for degenerate, virt'ous for virtuous, rev'rend for reverend. Also: "I had rather be a dog and bay the moon" (*JC*, IV, iii) (elide "I had" to "I'd"), or "Stir up the Athenian youth to merriments" (*MND*, I, i) (elide "Athenian" to "Athen'an"), or "An honest tale speeds best being plainly told" (*R3*, IV, iv) (elide "being" to "be'ng").

feminine ending—the unstressed eleventh syllable in a blank verse line, e.g., "To be, / or not / to be— / that is / the ques / tion:" (*Ham*, III, i).

iamb—a foot of two syllables, the first unstressed and the second stressed.

iambic pentameter—a verse line of five iambs, or ten syllables.

imagery—word pictures; mental images, e.g., "Gallop apace, you fiery-footed steeds," (*Rom*, iii, ii).

irony—the use of words to convey a meaning that is the opposite of its literal meaning (Webster), e.g., Mark Antony says to the crowd, "And Brutus is an honorable man." (*JC*, III, ii) Because of its double meaning, irony is always ambiguous.

metaphor—a figure of speech in which a term or phrase is applied to something to which it is not literally applicable in order to suggest a resemblance (Webster), e.g., "It is the East, and Juliet is the sun!" (*Rom*, II, i), or "Life's but a walking shadow, a poor player," (*Mac*, v, v).

meter—the measured arrangement of words into a specific pattern, e.g., lines of five feet (each foot is a meter), where each foot has two syllables.

onomatopoeia—a word made by imitation of a sound, e.g., "bang," "mock."

oxymoron—a figure of speech that is an impossible statement, usually an adjective modifying a contradictory noun, e.g., Romeo's "cold fire." (*Rom*, I, i)

pyrrhic—a foot consisting of two unstressed syllables back to back. A pyrrhic foot.

rhythm—the recurring pattern of strong and weak accents within the meter, e.g., dee dum, dee dum, dee dum, dee dum, dee dum.

scansion—analyzing and marking the metrical stresses and caesuras in a verse line.

simile—a figure of speech in which dissimilar things are compared using "like" or "as," e.g., "She would be as swift in motion as a ball;" (*Rom*, II, v), or "O sland'rous world! Kate like a hazel-twig/Is straight and slender, and as brown in hue/As hazel nuts and sweeter than the kernels." (The previous two lines include two similes and a metaphor.) (*Shr*, II, i), or "The quality of mercy is not strained;/It droppeth as the gentle rain from heaven" (*MV*, IV, i).

soliloquy—a solo speech, often delivered to the audience or camera.

spondee—a foot consisting of two equally stressed syllables. A spondaic foot. Example: "green light."

trochaic foot or *trochee*—a two-syllable foot, like the iamb, but with the first syllable stressed and the second unstressed. Often the first foot in a line, e.g., "Let me not think on't; frailty, thy name is woman—" (*Ham*, I, ii), or midline, e.g., "From ancient grudge, break to new mutiny" (*Rom*, Pro.).

Index

ABOUT THE AUTHOR

Wesley Van Tassel lived and studied in Minnesota, North Carolina, Denver, and New York City before beginning a fifteen-year stint as a director in the professional theatre. During this period, he served as artistic director of the Westport Playhouse, the Mule Barn Theatre, and the touring Continental Theatre Company. With a Ph.D. in dramatic literature, he then became a professor and has taught at four colleges/universities.

Wes has coached "acting Shakespeare" to several hundred professional and student actors, staged twenty-four AEA productions, produced fifty-five others, and directed more than one hundred summer or university productions.

Wes and his wife, actress Dude Hatten, live with their two dogs near Seattle. His son, Craig, lives in New York City, where he designs and engineers sound for Broadway shows. His son, Eric, who lives in Wyoming, is an artist whose primary emphasis is sculpture.

Wesley Van Tassel is available for stage and film voice and language coaching, one-semester or one-year visiting appointments in colleges or universities, or short-term workshop assignments in secondary schools or community theatres. He may be reached by e-mail at the publisher *PUB@allworth.com*, who will forward the message.

Books from Allworth Press

Promoting Your Acting Career
by Glenn Alterman (softcover, 6 × 9, 224 pages, $18.95)

Creating Your Own Monologue
by Glen n Alterman (softcover, 6 × 9, 192 pages, $14.95)

Technical Theater for Nontechnical People
by Drew Campbell (softcover, 6 × 9, 256 pages, $18.95)

An Actor's Guide—Your First Year in Hollywood, Revised Edition
by Michael Saint Nicholas (softcover, 6 × 9, 272 pages, $18.95)

Stage Fright: Health and Safety in the Theater
by Monona Rossol (softcover, 6 × 9, 144 pages, $16.95)

Booking and Tour Management for the Performing Arts
by Rena Shagan (softcover, 6 × 9, 272 pages, $19.95)

**Artists Communities: A Directory of Residencies in the United States
That Offer Time and Space for Creativity, Second Edition**
by the Alliance of Artists' Communities (softcover, 6³/₄ × 10, 240 pages, $18.95)

Your Modeling Career: You Don't Have to Be a Superstar to Succeed
by Debbie and Skip Press (softcover, 6 × 9, 256 pages, $14.95)

Selling Scripts to Hollywood
by Katherine Atwell Herbert (softcover, 6 × 9, 176 pages, $12.95)

Writing Scripts Hollywood Will Love
by Katherine Atwell Herbert (softcover, 6 × 9, 160 pages, $12.95)

The Songwriter's and Musician's Guide to Nashville
by Sherry Bond (softcover, 6 × 9, 256 pages, $18.95)

Making and Marketing Music
by Jodi Summers (softcover, 6 × 9, 240 pages, $18.95)

How to Pitch and Promote Your Songs, Revised Edition
by Fred Koller (softcover, 6 × 9, 192 pages, $18.95)

Please write to request our free catalog. To order by credit card, call 1-800-491-2808 or send a check or money order to Allworth Press, 10 East 23rd Street, Suite 210, New York, NY 10010. Include $5 for shipping and handling for the first book ordered and $1 for each additional book. Ten dollars plus $1 for each additional book if ordering from Canada. New York State residents must add sales tax.

To see our complete catalog on the World Wide Web, or to order online, you can find us at *www.allworth.com*.